TEXTS

Helmut Heissenbüttel

TEXTS

Selected and translated by
Michael Hamburger

MARION BOYARS
LONDON

A MARION BOYARS BOOK
distributed by Calder & Boyars Ltd
18 Brewer Street, London W1R 4AS

First published in Great Britain in 1977 by
Marion Boyars Publishers Ltd
18 Brewer Street, London W1R 4AS

All texts originally published in Germany. This selection taken from *Gelegenheitsgedichte und Klappentexte* (1973) and *Das Durchhauen des Kohlhaupts* (1974), published by Hermann Luchterhand Verlag, and from six *Textbücher* (1960-1967). Vols 1-5 published by Walter-Verlag. Vol 6 published by Hermann Luchterhand Verlag.

© Walter-Verlag and Luchterhand Verlag 1960-1967

© This selection and translation Michael Hamburger 1977

ALL RIGHTS RESERVED

ISBN 0 7145 2589 8 Cased edition
ISBN 0 7145 2590 1 Paper edition

Any paperback edition of this book whether published simultaneously with, or subsequent to, the cased edition is sold subject to the condition that it shall not, by way of trade, be lent, resold, hired out, or otherwise disposed of, without the publishers' consent, in any form of binding or cover other than that in which it is published.

No part of this publication may be reproduced, stored in a retrieval system, or transmitted, in any form or by any means, electronic, mechanical, photocopying, recording or otherwise, except brief extracts for the purposes of review, without the prior written permission of the copyright owner and publisher.

Printed in Great Britain by Villiers Publications Ltd, London.
Bound in Great Britain by Hunter & Foulis Ltd, Edinburgh.

CONTENTS

Introduction   9

Combination VII   17
Combination XI   18
Window contents   19
Fragment III   20
Interior   21
Pamphlets (1954)   22
Topographies (1954)   27
Simple sentences   29
Simple grammatical meditations (1955)   30

from Would-Be Novel

A room in my flat   35
Allegory   37
In transit between two situations   38
I the murdered   39
The water painter   41
Talking with the doctrinaire   43
Variations on the opening of a novel   45
Novel   48
Treatise   50
Situation   51
The most considerate person in the world   52
Grammatical reduction   55
Political grammar   56

from Generalization

Wedding reception   59
Blackcurrants   60
Tourist season   62

from 3 x 13 More-Or-Less Stories

Schematic development of a tradition   65
Social contract   67
Final solution   68
Catalogue of the incorrigible   70
Short story   71
A simple story   72
Family politics   74
Bremen whereyou   76
Bremen where you   76
Bad news   78
The question of identity   80
Explanation of the rhinoceros   82
Class analysis   86
The new age   87
The future of socialism   88
So what   90
The dilemma of being high and dry   92

from New Treatises on Human Understanding

A 45-year-old Englishwoman from Birmingham   95
Germany 1944   100

from Occasional Poems and Blurbs

Occasional poem no. 6   107

from The Splitting of the Cabbage

Max immediately before falling asleep   111

INTRODUCTION

More than any living writer I can think of, Helmut Heissenbüttel deserves to be called an experimental writer; not in the loose sense that makes 'experimental' a synonym for 'modern' or 'avant-garde' — pretty useless and meaningless categories in any case — but in the sense that his work is a continuous experiment with words and sentences, conducted in a manner as nearly scientific as his various media permit. Whether the processes and methods he applies to language are new matters less than the rigour and consistency with which he applies them. Collage, montage, simultaneity, tautology, grammatical dislocation and permutation — all these had been used before, by the Dadaists, by Gertrude Stein, by a host of early twentieth century innovators whose precedent Heissenbüttel has freely acknowledged in his critical writings or in his own texts. As I pointed out in *The Truth of Poetry*, one of these precedents — the grammatical *perpetuum mobile* adopted again and again by Heissenbüttel in his *3 x 13 mehr oder weniger Geschichten* and elsewhere — can be traced back as far as Tristan Corbière's *Les Amours Jaunes*, published in 1873. Again, it matters very little whether or not this particular epigraph by Corbière, a mere *jeu d'esprit* to him, with no sequel in his practice, served Heissenbüttel as a model for his method. What is certain is that Heissenbüttel's method is applied to altogether different material, and produces altogether different results. The cult of novelty for novelty's sake is bound up with an individualism that Heissenbüttel's practice has left behind.

'Anti-grammatical, anti-syntactical transformation and reproduction of language,' Heissenbüttel wrote for his Frankfurt lectures, 'are effective principles in twentieth century literature. Leaving aside that part of linguistic reproduction which can be interpreted in terms of social themes or cultural criticism, both principles, like their advocates, are described in current critical jargon as experimental (and it is quite conceivable that this could lead to the classification of the whole period as experimental, much as earlier periods are classified as "baroque" or "romantic"). Personally I regard the concept of experimental literature as a product of educational politics, a tactical resort, with no factual validity. Yet it can be used as a means of making oneself understood. Contrary to the usual tacit assumption, this notion of experimental literature does not stand in opposition to a so-called "normal" literature. Beside it there is only one other literary principle, that of stylization or pseudo-stylization. In many cases experimental and stylizing literature have formed alliances that make for complexity, but often also for perplexity, as soon as we apply those principles to specific works.'

There are traces of individual stylization still in Heissenbüttel's early texts, especially those in the collection *Kombinationen*. Although he has not seen fit to reprint this first collection, or to include any part of it in his later 'textbooks', I have included a few pieces from it as a point of departure for the later experiments. These first texts look more or less like lyrical poems; but they are lyrical poems pervaded by the awareness that this lyricism is threatened by a drastic discontinuity. Heterogeneous prosaic reflections and perceptions intrude. Heissenbüttel's break with lyricism was gradual and inevitable. It developed from the awareness that lyrical poetry, as practised right up to our time by poets whom Heissenbüttel does not necessarily reject but found it impossible to emulate, is held together by a subjectivity that avails itself of objective or symbolic correlatives to create an order. This order, to Heissenbüttel, became an illusion or, as he calls it, a hallucination.

What makes his early texts recognizably 'poetic' is not that they are divided into verse lines — so are many of his later texts — far less that they fall into rhyme at times, but that they have not broken with subjectivity to the point of ceasing to register experiences and perceptions that disrupt or threaten it. For that reason they remain self-expressive, even confessional, in a way that the later texts are not. By this I don't mean that autobiographical material is not used in the later texts, but that it becomes material of the same order as any other, used not for self-expression but for experiments with language. More and more, it is the verbal processes that count. These verbal processes, in turn, serve to reveal possibilities of meaning, possibilities of truth, inherent in language itself, rather than in the individual consciousness and sensibility that we expect to meet in the poems, short stories, novels and plays of writers less austerely, less rigorously experimental.

Helmut Heissenbüttel was born in 1921 in Wilhelmshaven. His father, the son of a village carpenter, spent twelve years in the German Navy before taking civilian employment and contributing essays to the local paper. Heissenbüttel served in the army, and was seriously wounded on active service in 1941, losing his left arm. In the later war years he studied architecture, history of art and German, completing his studies in Hamburg after the war, and working there for some years as a publisher's reader. Since 1959 he has been a radio producer in Stuttgart. His early books *Kombinationen* and *Topographien* were published in 1954. Between 1960 and 1967 his work appeared in six 'textbooks', collected into one volume in 1970. These were followed in 1970 by the novel *D'Alemberts Ende*, a collection of 'occasional poems and blurbs' (1970)—the latter written for exhibition catalogues—and by a collection of dialogues, mainly for radio, *das durchhauen des kohlhaupts* (1974). Heissenbüttel's critical and theoretical writings were collected in the volumes *Über Literatur* (1966), *Briefwechsel über Literatur* (with Heinrich Vormweg) (1969) and *Zur Tradition der Moderne* (1972). Heissenbüttel has been active, too. as a sponsor of the work of many other writers and artists, contributing critical appreciations not only to exhibition catalogues but to a whole series of books by poets and prose writers. His Frankfurt lectures on poetics, delivered in 1963, were published in the volume *Über Literatur*.

Almost from the start Heissenbüttel tended as much towards narrative prose as towards poetry, writing 'quasi-stories' and 'quasi-novels' long before his full-length novel was published. Just as his poems questioned the presuppositions of lyrical poetry, his miniature quasi-novels and quasi-stories questioned the presuppositions of narrative fiction. Miniature quasi-dramas are the most recent extension of his range, though these too follow from earlier experiments and are best described by the neutral term 'texts', because, as Heissenbüttel wrote in 1963, 'the development of the arts in the twentieth century shows this characteristic, among others, that it advances sporadically into areas where every genre comes up against the frontier of every other'. Not only do his texts cross the frontiers between poetry, prose fiction and drama, but they are as closely bound up with developments in the visual arts and in music as with developments in literature; and his methods are inseparable from the philosophical and linguistic interests evident in everything he has written.

One does not need to refer back to the 'two cultures' debate to point out that most of the 'avant-garde' literature of an earlier period, including that of Dadaism, was anti-philosophical, anti-theoretical, anti-methodical. Though Heissenbüttel can be playful, high-spirited and funny, it is the austerity of his aims and methods that makes many of his texts difficult to read. They make little concession to the pleasure principle — unless it is the pleasure that a mathematician or logician may take in a piece of work thoroughly and efficiently carried to its conclusion. They also demand a kind of concentration that little contemporary writing demands, and less of it gets; for we expect imaginative literature to grip us, move us, carry us away — hallucinate us, in fact, to a greater or lesser degree — whereas most of Heissenbüttel's later texts are meant to exercise the intellect by jolting it out of its habits and assumptions. Those habits and assumptions are not only reflected, but embodied, in the way we speak — in idioms, phrases, grammatical structures; and it is these that Heissenbüttel's texts shake up, often simply by letting them reduce themselves to absurdity. The end of Heissenbüttel's art is enlightenment; and enlightenment brought about without recourse to persuasion, appeal to emotional stock responses, or any of the traditional devices of didactic art. Many of his texts are abstract and general to a degree we associate with science and philosophy rather than with imaginative art. Even the visual particulars of which they are full assume a function less sensuous than exemplary, just as the characters in them assume a function less individual than algebraic.

'In these developments,' to quote Heissenbüttel again on twentieth century poetics, 'method takes on a strong preponderance. He who can grasp it can use it. One can imagine a state of affairs in which what is methodical about this literature could indeed become general. The arrested exemplars serve for the study of methods. The question of quality will lose its validity, as will the question of poetry (as something more elevated), of art. Success will depend not on a particular gift (the Muse's kiss) but on an attitude to language (or other media) that can be taken by anyone. The consistency of methods that decipher language, reproduce language, duplicate a language-world, is not due to its needing the subjectivity of the poet who, as it were, attracts all other subjects to himself to make literature, but to the method's ability to provide something that can be used by anyone who avails himself of it. There is a possibility (and this, though only a hypothesis, is not idle speculation) that the thing we still have to call literature will become general. That the old dream of the universal language of literature can be fulfilled, not by regression to pseudo-humanistic and pseudo-subjective clichés, as dogmatic Communist culture ideology and the restorative culture-preservers of the West would have it, but by the practice of post-subjective progressive literary methods.'

That utopia or science fiction, depending on how we look at it, has not come closer to fulfilment in the fourteen years that have passed since those words were written; and I for one can't pretend that I'm sorry. An element of personal choice, I note with relief, enters even into Heissenbüttel's most rigorously methodical exercises; and even a scientist's experiments are based on hypotheses or hunches, sometimes on flashes which in poets would be called inspiration. I confess to being moved by some of Heissenbüttel's texts, such as his re-interpretation of the Job story, *bad news*, in which method is less obtrusive, less autonomous, than elsewhere. Heissenbüttel may let grammar have its head, but it is he who harnesses it to the original proposition which it will pull from stage to stage, he who provides the fodder and the load. It is also he who must know or have a good idea in advance not perhaps exactly where grammar's career will lead, but what kind of profit — psychological, sociological or ontological — any one trip is likely to yield. His methods have been available for a long time, but no one else has made them work quite as he makes them work. So I suspect that there never will be such a thing as a 'general Literature', practicable by anyone who has grasped the methods, if only because not everyone has the desire or equipment; and Heissenbüttel's equipment, his knowledge, intelligence and skill, is as distinctive as his dedication to literature as 'a means of radical enlightenment'. This is not the place to go into the other reasons, or to point out what severe limitations and losses literature would suffer if it were to become a branch of technology. Those implications can be left to Heissenbüttel's readers.

Of the present selection I need say no more than that it is intended to be representative of Heissenbüttel's range, within the limits of translatability. Of the pieces I was unable to translate I especially regret his *Gedicht über die Ubung zu sterben* (1962-3); and it may be that I, or the linguistic resources available to me, have shown some bias towards texts in which Heissenbüttel's investigations produce satirical effects, or texts anchored in recognizable situations. The translations are as literal as I could make them. Since language, to a considerable though not absolute degree, is Heissenbüttel's subject, his texts leave scarcely any scope for transposition or paraphrase; and the sort of imitation they permit would be wholly independent compositions applying Heissenbüttel's processes to other verbal material. It may well be that such imitations would prove more satisfactory than literal versions. If so, one function of these translations could be to make the processes more widely known.

Michael Hamburger

COMBINATION VII

1
Time is bitter.
But in this hole in the clouds burns the green stone of transformation.
Coloured planes glide through abstract scaffolding.

2
NOSTALGIA.
The landscape of words shows combinations
Beyond the range of invention.

3
Strange life:
Fragments of a text into which all the time
Other fragments are inserted.
But which is the true text?

4
Autumn hands winter leaf.
Fine days are processed like butterflies for collectors.

5
And leaf after leaf falls
Down on to dark earth
That offers them all
Its wide-open mouth.

COMBINATION XI

1
The night is a pattern of arclights and rearlights of cars.
On the Alster's unstirring plane stand the white flags of night.
Shadows move under the trees.
It is I.

2
Darkroom conversations.
Darkroom memory.
Shadow mesh over thawing ice.
The embankment lights balance on mirror stilts.
The unlighted places are wilting.

3
All these sentences.
The inventory of occasions.
Don't forget.
Jabber of gramophone records.
The memory of sound tracks on reels put away.

4
And the questions are the sentences that I cannot speak.
And the thoughts are the birds that fly off and do not return.

WINDOW CONTENTS

What is touching about the November evening, for example.
Geometry of the vertically obstructed walls beyond the courtyard.
Clothesline physiognomy of the balcony.
The watercolour daubs of the sky.
Brushes of the shadow-trees.
Or simply the vertical drop of sparrow feathers.
The picture of the cut-out rectangle is comforting.
The consolation of visibility.

FRAGMENT III

All horizons are round.
On the plain's flat disc I am
The centre of remote church spires.

The voice on the radio says
FREEDOM IS AN IMPOSSIBLE THING.
After that
String Quartet No. 4 by Arnold Schoenberg.

INTERIOR

Hats Picasso photographs pile of books
paper flowers from the party of the year before last
cowrie shells Chinese buttons a bronze lizard
the calendar with the dates of days that have passed
dice cup and patience cards
dumped by the years
dumped by the years that I was

PAMPHLETS

I
the present rehearses its liturgy—a manner of speaking grown vain
                                                                  faded quotations
thoughts without feet discover those melancholy adverbial qualifi-
                                                                   cations [clauses]
  the lyrics of song hits outlast their time
  the bride of the stranded window rains in a dream
  and the dark room's mandolins move to and fro
  other years intrude
  depression's architecture trembles above these occasional canals
  out of ripped perspectives hang the naked breasts of long ago

II
my biblical history begins with the smell of the moors in August
my paleolithic age reaches only as far as my childhood
prosody of railway trucks
the discontinuous passage of time
yesterday was three weeks ago
grapes of days hang on the past's exterior
my disquiet is the sight of water divided by rowing boats
my disquiet is the sound of dice rolling over the top of my desk
angles of vision snap over my face askance

III [mottos]
the light is like a nude and carefully depilated woman
soon they will speak of silence as of a fairy tale
to be charmed seemed enough ambition for anyone with sense
the business of life is to make a solitude that is not loneliness
stance: that of a man not in agreement even with himself
all sentences have the same value
la tristesse rembourse

IV
the bad old era couples with the new era and engenders old opinions
horrible memories walk about empty-handed
on woman's hour Nietzsche is proved wrong
Adolf Hitler is a character in Michaux
families are being worn
the pasts of ministers flirt
over laughing faces the shadow-columns of H-bomb explosions slowly
                                                                                                      pass
car models move representatively through let's call them districts
the new era rises and sets like the evening star in September

V [from newspapers]
the possibility of recognition could be demonstrated perhaps
unanimous recognition would be one position
altogether if under all circumstances
circumstances from which it follows
in such a manner that
the optional inferences relevant to the case
in certain respects it is a matter of possibilities perpetually increasing
in certain respects a hopeless position would be a possibility

VI
I go straight ahead
I do not go straight ahead
I declare myself in agreement
I declare myself not in agreement
I tell the truth
I do not tell the truth
I recognize
I disrecognize
I assert
I talk
I do not talk

VII
ink blots hurriedly flee over the blueprint of the September evening
a Miró of 1931 with the title Silence
the fountain of swallows is on its way
the desk lamp solves no riddles
in vain the Miró extends its arm from Heidegger to Wittgenstein
the yellow rainlight of the September evening sticks to the window-
                                                                                                     pane
the yellow arms of the September evening clasp me to them
the yellow September light of the rainy evening noiselessly strikes
                                                    home like a shot made of silence

VIII
here the large blue butterflies rest
spreadings out that occurred in the inaudible
here the green balconies of my prehistory land
glossed areas wander slowly through unknown parts of the city
the black poplars bend over one another and fall silent
dead bicycles roll slowly through the forgetful world
empty windows move in wide ranks over the soundless landscape
? what do the empty windows look for?

IX [for Kurt Leonhard]
weary with the grimace of putting oneself forward
inaccessible on the roundabout of recurrent opportunities
neighbouring on the noises of railway stations
beyond all the possible partings
unrecognized within the obligingness of human intercourse
transient in the hope of reunion
hypothetically at hand
because experiment is the only guarantee
because experiment is the only proof

X
the laughing faces have all been given a new coat of paint
for this is the way of the world
the laughing faces are all wearing new clothes
so the contentedness of the world can be proved
be positive people say
enquire in the leading specialist shops
have them show you the splendid new models at such low prices
the laughing faces are collapsible

XI
in the rain of this October night in 1954 the façade of never meeting
                                                                                 again waits motionless
over these faces shedding their leaves the picture sequences of the
                                                                         train windows hover like clouds
it has not come back
punctuation of the sun gone down
time shines like a child's lantern vanished in the dark
and even the stories that can be told have died
it has not returned

XII [words of comfort]
the plane that is before you will gradually turn white
the impassable three-dimensional corners will stick together
more closely your face will draw forgetfulness round its shoulders
lips distorted with weeping will get up and go
what we called being happy
the shallow bowl of anxiety will silently rise like smoke
the wind with no smell will extend its hand

XIII
irregularly the black mills distribute themselves over my theme
motionless the blue figures of conjecture stand in the dark like
                                                                         reflections in water
the occasionally visible black desks of thoughts that have reached
                                                                                   their end
the walls are covered with the moon's graffiti
the disquiet over the fact that there was an AS or a WB
in the midst of movements made by heart rises the rejecting lemon
                                                                      odour Never Yet
on the horizon pricking its ears hang the ships' sirens of departure
among the possible variations glitter the castanets of silence
right in your ear the soundless gong of October explodes

TOPOGRAPHIES

a
breathlessly the birds of world history cross the bare tracts
irreparable things shocks shameless hussy losses
Big Sid Catlett Art Tatum Fats Navarro
recall of the underground of my landscape
for I a novel by Gustav Freytag
single white patches quickly moving across the visible contours
a white gull detaches itself from the profile of the fleeting
faces fallen away on the steps of the underground shafts
the faces of the dead
in rushing haste the night's radiation points multiply
rusty box-shapes swing slowly despairingly irresistibly into the
                                              steel-blue protecting
  layer

b
time
prehistory dwindles to future
between the russet October trees the lemon-yellow motor cars move
the blackish beauty of a hydrangea mummy
the slow pace of those who expect nothing
loss of time
the cessation of identity on the bridge
traces of aniseed in the air
doors of aniseed
death is so permanent
the brass rods of time-consciousness blindly collide

c
incessantly the same faces meet in the stream made to flow in opposite
directions
the loudspeakers talk uniterruptedly
the little girl's piano-playing drives a tunnel through the years
the cry of the gull that slices my early dreams is still my sister
from the tunnels the illuminated façades rise up
wood fire sky of the remoter regions
open doors to disused railway trucks in the November sun
flattened smoke tracts over marshalling yards
meshed mirror images in the corrugated iron of canals
in this canal and this region of bridges
the glittering parallels of the tract in front of me

d
subtract days count annoyances function precisely
without interest in the interests of interested parties
that with the thing that can be achieved less is achieved than when
nothing is achieved
being seduced again and again to the same sort of sentences
hiding-place Benjamin Peret and Francis Picabia
brain-waves transferred
surviving thoughts
everything differs from its hypothesis
the truth is my memory
I collect passers-by who talk to themselves
I signify the absence of thoughts in faces that have fallen away

e
sentences without content in the night's drift
real nocturnal snatches of conversation in trams
voices over the ice
the deserted face that I recognize
one day before Christmas
nightland night-blue
winged wandering of the night
the milk-brown circular shape
now
now now now

SIMPLE SENTENCES

as I stand my shadow falls
the first drawing is sketched by the morning sun
to flower is a deadly occupation
I have declared myself to be in agreement
I live

SIMPLE GRAMMATICAL MEDITATIONS

a [tautologies]
the shadow that I cast is the shadow that I cast
the situation into which I have got is the situation into which I have got
the situation into which I have got is yes and no
situation my situation my special situation
groups of groups move across empty planes
groups of groups move across pure colours
groups of groups move across the shadow that I cast
the shadow that I cast is the shadow that I cast
groups of groups move across the shadow that I cast and vanish

b
the blackness of the water and the punctuality of the lights
the blackness of the water and the occasionalness of the reflections
regions and regions and landscapes
landscapes that I have coloured and landscapes that I have not
                                                                                 coloured
the occasionalness of the shadows and the chromaticism of bright
                                                                                    things
the blackness of black things and the chromaticism of bright patches
yellow red yellowish red and red red red
regions and landscapes and or
or and or or

c [subjunctive]
up to the middle of the half
less than too little
least of all
as though as though
probably probably
took upon himself did not take upon himself
undecided
provisionally provisional

d
iron-hatching of mirrorings and reflections and afternoons
afternoons and afternoons and afternoons
afternoons are more current than pasts
afternoons are not more frequent than pasts
the afternoon by which I denote is more denotable than pasts
slowly receded afternoons through a cross-hatching of mirrorings
goings-on that have gone away refer
cracked mirror surfaces and afternoons more cracked
afternoons more cracked and afternoons more cracked

e
small black verticals intersect slow black horizontals
rain-shaped things intersect rain-shaped things
squads of walls
small black sad rectangles incessantly roaming
hesitant diagonals
finite straight lines intersecting
in any case in the given case I talk talk
talk intersects talk and there is there is not not
talk intersects talk and there is there is no such thing none and never
                                                                                                   never

f [participial]
waiting waiting to have waited
to be waited
brought round not brought round to have been brought round
retracted retractions
noises stretched across
noises stretched across from finite points of time
retracted retractions retractable directed at
erected directed at an erected direction
erected directions from infinite points of time

FROM *WOULD-BE NOVEL*

A ROOM IN MY FLAT

There is a room in my flat that I hardly knew. I had even once played with the possibility of having its doorway bricked in and papered. Now that I'm in it and can't get out again I try in vain to remember exactly where in my flat this room is situated. I have looked in vain for a plan. There is none. Or else it got lost. And when I think I remember that this room was an outside room that assumption is contradicted by everything I see and I am even tempted to say that it's right at the centre of my flat [and walled up it would have become a sort of hollow].

True, the room has windows. Windows and then again no windows one might say. Cut-out spaces it might be more accurate to say that appear in different places on the wall and vanish again. Almost like pictures. [Rainy street in the afternoon or at night a row of street lights or the face behind a window-pane and many other things.] Possibly there are doors too. Could it be that I only haven't found them yet? [Not even the one through which I got in?] As I sit here I try to remember how I got in. On the whole I'm still inclined to regard it as an accident. The doorlock had worked loose. The door was ajar. I pushed it. I hesitated. Then went in. I'm always trying now to understand what made me hesitate. It wasn't caution or fear far less a premonition. For the room attracted me. A sort of reunion. A sense of return. And curiosity too. And yet I hesitated?

I recall that I was planning something when I entered the room. Nothing remains of those plans. I don't even remember what sort of plans they could have been. Instead I tried to explore the room. I learned it by heart as it were complete with its inventory. But I realized that this wasn't what was needed. Ever since I've been sitting here staring in front of me or at the pictures of windows that appear on the walls and without feeling the movement of my tongue I think I started to talk and at first heard only the tone the incessantly murmuring complaining unfamiliar tone of the unintelligible and evilly [so it seemed to me] cajoling voice that was my own. My own strange voice.

Since I first heard that voice I've known that I'm like a man who has succeeded in buying the very thing he had previously sold and who now tries to find out with the help of nothing but that commodity how it came about. Who doesn't know whether he wants to keep the thing he can't give away. Who still believes that tomorrow will refute what today proved. Who doesn't believe in any evidence unless it is in anger. Who perhaps is already beginning to disparage what he wanted more than anything to find. A few hours ago I discovered that there is a mirror in the room. Evidently I discovered it because I was looking for doors again. I was exhausted. I looked up. I saw a face. A tired face a tiredly and listlessly observing face. Tiredly and listlessly observing eyes. Once those eyes had been hopeful once those eyes had been angry. All this had passed without changing anything.

I remember the idea I conceived and it's the same idea I still have now for this is a report and not a story. If ever I shall be in a position [I'm thinking] to leave this room I shall give up my flat and go away no matter where or how. I think that and at the same time I think that I shall never again leave this room even if I were in a position to leave it but shall stay in it for ever and ever.

Variant: When they found him he was lying behind the only door. It was open. It had always been open.

ALLEGORY

I had submerged. Vertically I hung over the shadow of that which was no more. Green time. The bottom was pebbly and bright and full of little weeds and shifting shadows. Shifting green cool light. Pleasantly cool light after the glaring illumination of that which was. Swaying silence of dissolved duration. Not to last longer. The loveliest days of my dying. Without event or expectation.
Before I submerged I had thought of this state as the final liberation. But it was only the conditional absence of actual things. No longer involved absconded vanished.
In this curious aquarium of my emotional contents a dead man. Already it strikes home again. Never ceases to strike home. Hurls me forward. That I had submerged meant nothing more than that I had submerged. No more. I had forgotten the larger fishes. Now they are assembled. Hanging over the shadow vertically I swing with their butting. Now they assault me in shoals led by the fattest and blackest from the least likely corner of that forgotten cellar. Green nothingness filled by the furious butting of the beaters. Green twilight transformed by the foaming bubbling beating of their fins. Soundless jellyfish of swollen nostalgia. Did I really come here of my own accord? Everything there was before my coming here takes on a benign colouring. At the impact of those ever more violent blows my head gradually detaches itself. At times under gentle blows it already moves on its own. Will they be satisfied when they have it?

IN TRANSIT BETWEEN TWO SITUATIONS

The first situation lies some way back on the left. It is round and open. Yellow and smooth inside and rough black cracked outside. Appears to stand on something that is fragile. Seems fragile itself. [But broken would probably be different.] Contains something. Balls of paper perhaps. Envelopes it could be or wrapping paper. Used up stuff. Crumbs refuse peelings.

The second situation looks like a bridge. A bridge I have crossed either once or innumerable times. One could describe it too as a shallow arc a connecting line between one side and the other. Something above something. Phrases excuses claims. Between the wings of the time of day and seasons. But not a bridge. Something stuck together knotted. Something that can be undone.

In transit between two situations I see a window shining through the night. [Always the same route. Small bare trees. Wind that opposes rain that lashes the face. I walk. As I walk the route moves always in the same direction as I and I never reach my destination. Everything remains as near and as far as before.]

Rooms that disappear at the edges. Wide shallow rooms with no bounds. A floor and a ceiling nothing more. A searchlight moves to and fro. For moments it pauses quivering. Slips and somersaults. Then back on the ceiling. A round yellow rotating disc. And when the disc gradually fades out a knocking footfall approaches from the depths. Wanders about. Comes closer. Stops becomes more menacing. Swells and while in the swelling roar the rooms begin to quake the searchlight returns sharp glaring bounded and leaps in between. Playing together round each other the searchlight and the knocking ghost now make off from echo to echo.

I THE MURDERED

I was murdered in the last Cawnpore uprising. In those terrible days of the uprising I was lured by two men into a house and killed.
                              [Indian newspaper report]

When they found me I was lying under a board floor and a layer of cement. They were a boy and a girl. The girl was cross-eyed. She had ripped up the floorboards and broken the cement with a pick. I remembered nothing.
They had found me in the newspaper kiosk. How did they guess that I could be lying there? How had they hit on the idea of digging me up? Were they looking for something else [or nothing]? It was me they had found.
They were talking. At first I couldn't understand what they said. At first I wasn't interested in what they said. They stood close to the wall. The girl turned to the boy looked at him. He had lowered his head. What were they planning? Did they want to remove me? Did they want to leave me there?
Perhaps they were trying to discover the truth. The truth [I know it now] was that I had returned to daylight. That was irrevocable. They had murdered me. They had buried me. But I was still there. A boy and a cross-eyed girl had dug me up. Perhaps they guessed what they had done. But if they guessed they didn't know [I assume] what consequences that act could have. Or did they? Was that what they were talking about?
Suddenly he walked across the hut towards me and stared at me. We've found him [he said] that's the one. Stick him back in [she called out] we'll have nothing but trouble with him. Leave him lying where he is. — He can't vanish completely [said the boy] now that we've found him. — Take him out then stand him up and say it was us [she screamed]. Yes [he said] why not us.
I began to remember. It was hard. Even if I was well preserved [I was well preserved] that was something different and didn't mean anything. For time had passed. [A summer evening with the noise of passing convoys of trucks [something like that?] street smells and footsteps invisible in the dark suddenly the loudspeaker's voice a light quickly leaping by in the foliage of trees [what trees?] rainy wind wind

that smells of rain and the torso of a grey raincoat]? [rhododendron? garden railings?]

The boy and the girl were now at the door. They stared out through the newspapers hung up there. Were they waiting? What for? Couldn't they make up their minds? To do what? To take their chance? Was I their chance? Still? O God still.

I remember the shadows against the brighter night sky. Then a streaking shadow [of a bird or bullet?] Noiselessly quickly passing. The same one? Something lighting up. Always gone again at once noiselessly too. A hand [?] moving fast. Fast? Or slowly?

There was a smell of earth. It had been easier than I expected. No sweat a single spasm of the heart and no meaningless phrases. Suddenly wind is excitedly shaking about here and there. Murmuring the sound rises. The wind has gone. Quietly. So quietly. Something had come to an end. Once and for all. I was dead. Not so dead that I couldn't be dug up again. But dead all the same. A well-preserved corpse. Here was the next generation or the one after. It had dug me up. In a newspaper kiosk. Was it a sensation for them to have dug me up? There was a noise in the street. The door opened. Shadows came in. Torches. A loud voice. Calls. They surrounded me. The girl stared at the boy. He had stuck his hands in his pockets.

They took hold of me. They took hold of me and lifted me up and carried me away. While they were carrying me away the girl asked: You did telephone? He didn't answer. He spat out something from between his teeth and followed the crowd. We found him! [the girl shrieked] and she extended her open hands with the fingers spread.

They carried me away and began to use me up. Burying was not safe enough. Murdered people can be found again. They preserved me and are using me up. They're etching away at me as at a pencil drawing. They've got pretty far.

THE WATER PAINTER

He painted on water. That was his invention.
He painted on water that is: he didn't let coloured water run over paper like earlier painters. He didn't paint pictures for hanging up. He didn't paint pictures at all. Not what had been called pictures before his invention.
He painted on water. On all kinds of water. On rain puddles and lakes on the surfaces of filled saucepans. On overflowed water around a vase. On sea water. On bath water. He painted on smooth water. He painted on rough water. On clear water and on murky water full of algae and deposits. Shadows and sun reflections. Even coloured water if it was available. Never [as uninitiated people might have supposed] on any other kind of liquid. It had to be water.
Sometimes he wasn't satisfied with what was at hand and he went on long journeys to find the right water. Sometimes he made do with the next best thing. It happened that a spotty flooded desk top enchanted him. It happened that he needed this one mountain lake between dark wooded slopes. Sometimes he was content to paint kneeling on the shore on the pebbles or lying on a landing-stage. Sometimes he rowed for hours to find the right light the right solitude. For a time he used a raft with a square cut out in the middle. He used several methods when painting. Usually he had various sorts of sticks. Apart from them he needed boards rubber discs hair-brushes combs fly-swatters and paintbrushes. Sometimes compass and ruler. These had a special fascination for him at one time. He could be seen among the breakers or a heavy turbulent sea in thunderstorms applying cleanly executed straight lines and far-flung arcs for hours. He painted with his fingers and with his spread hands. With his feet and even with his whole body.
He rarely used colours. If so he let the colour drip into flowing water or drew it through with paintbrushes and sticks. He would pour in colour by the bucketful. Once he used a fountain pen.
His pictures. They weren't pictures as mentioned before. Games made of curve wave reflection shadow of traces and traces of traces. Once when he tried to complement water painting [he too didn't want to get stuck in a rut] with shadow modelling he suffered a relapse. After going on from combinations of plain shadows and coloured shadows

he caught himself beginning to photograph his shadow modelling at one of its changing stages. That was his relapse. To preserve hold fast pass on exhibit all these were a relapse. They were the useless thing. After that he remained idle for a time. Possibly he wanted to punish himself by desisting. Possibly too something was surging up inside him out of this relapse to a purer mode of imagining. True in that case his progress would have remained imperceptible. But after an interval of seeming or real apathy he began again to paint on water. Only a very careful observer [there wasn't one] could have noticed slight changes in him. A brief hesitancy in the midst of a stroke. A more hurried departure from water to water. A stopping in work scarcely begun.

TALKING WITH THE DOCTRINAIRE

I
[asked me yesterday and I answered said I know (later I admitted by way of conversation that I don't know) said I am for it I am not for it what annoys me about the business is that]

II
I speak. I have opinion no opinion several opinion many opinion. Things which according to my opinon I know something about. Things which according to my opinion I know nothing about. Things with which I have concerned myself and things with which I have not concerned myself. About which I have heard something about which I have heard nothing about which I have read something or seen something or not etc.

III
Do you consider that your attitude is right? Do you consider that you are right to take that attitude? Don't you consider that you should take a different attitude? Don't you consider that you could take a different attitude? I take an attitude or I don't take an atttiude. I take a decision or I don't take a decision. I commit myself or I don't commit myself. [Did you support Adenauer? Do you go to the cinema? Are you keen on jazz? Would you stand up for homosexuals? Do you think that the man in the street has any use for modern art? Are you happily married? Do you smoke filter cigarettes?]

IV
I am there. [The unpleasant thing is that one can't avoid getting involved if one is there.] I don't know what I'm getting involved in. Or I do know and don't want to or I do not want to but don't know whether that in which I'm getting involved won't have turned into something different when I am involved in it. One can go into details and give reasons for everything one can go into details and divert everything one can go into details and dissect everything. Inregardto inrelationto dependingon etc. One can also [of course] leave all that alone.

V

[For instance I jumped on the bandwagon. I was predisposed to jumping on the bandwagon. But I didn't know what it was. I wanted to get to know. What I got to know was what jumping on the bandwagon means. When I got to know what it means to jump on the bandwagon I stopped. In certain circumstances I even became useless because I know what it means. But in other circumstances I became more useful because I know what it means to jump on the bandwagon.]

VI

[Or one informs oneself. Gathers arranges cuts out chooses connects surveys observes perceives perceives perception accepts perception registers registers systematically destroys the system and registers the destruction and doesn't stop and informs oneself in that way. Informs oneself all round in a definite direction without direction in a backward direction too in a forward direction too etc.]

VII

I speak. I rattle on. Take no notice whether anyone is listening. Assume that there are listeners that there is this one or anyone or any group of people. What I speak is not commitments answers acknowledgements denials. What I speak is not opinions. [My opinion is always the same.] What I speak is what is sayable. What is sayable? Something. What is sayable means I make myself understood without considering whether I am understandable. Or being misunderstood. [When I am understood I am always understood correctly.] My consideration consists in that I assume that the inconsiderateness of my making myself understood makes the non-understandable [the seemingly non-understandable] understandable.

VIII

Wrapped up in meshes of opinion and proverbs and all such camp-following stuff. All this camp-following stuff that I drag along behind me. If I stir everything is at once stirred also whole areas of stuff dragged along are set into motion. Whole areas of stuff dragged along become language ever new areas are set in motion ever new areas become language. All this ensnares me. Becomes tangled. Tautens. Tenses tears drags hangs. I keep still and everything moves through me. I lie down and everything moves over me. Do I participate in it at all? Groping I signal my way through the stuff dragged along. I signal my way on.

VARIATIONS ON THE OPENING OF A NOVEL

I

He was still disappointed. Only one side of this street had lamps. They had already been lit. He looked for a street sign. When he got to it he could not decipher it. It was deathly quiet. There are streets like this [he thought] in every city with more than a certain number of inhabitants. As he walked on he thought: Either people here go to bed at this early hour or it's later than I thought or the houses are empty. A patch of light appeared on one of the grey walls and went out before he had reached it. There was a stench of fish or something that reminded him of sculleries. The street was on a gentle slope. Cobbles with narrow brick borders. Ended ahead of him in the air. A rectangle with only three sides. Wall pavement wall. Above them nothing. Sky. Dun-coloured sky just resolved to darken.

II

A person. Personal pronoun third person singular masculine. A figure? The hero of a story? Someone to whom something is happening [or has happened]? Centre of a situation a story a plot? Tension: something has already happened. He is still disappointed. Eventualities that offer themselves. What could have happened if. Narrate? He is still disappointed. His disappointment hasn't abated. Endures is stubborn does not diminish but rather is confirmed. Is almost a trait of character almost an action.

III

Very much like identifying a photograph when one has forgotten whom it depicts. Identify what? The point is that there must have been an original. Can't a picture have been freely invented? But the presupposition is that it has not been freely invented. Can't it have been an unusually vivid dream? It could have been one of those dreams for instance that one dreamed when [when what?]. Or what good would it do one if one knew: Rouen June 18 1940 10.30 p.m. Somewhere it seems the specific detail must be accommodated as a part. If only as the supposition of a part. If only as the pure fiction of a part.

IV

On both sides shadows emerge from the dark. Momentary tunnels of momentary searchlights. Almost without a sound. Black leaves on black branches. Now pressed to the wall. It had caught up with him. Or had he caught up with it? Now he remembered. Right the voice had said that he remembered now. Was it right? Everything was right. Everyone was right. One couldn't do anything. He was still disappointed.

V

He was still disappointed.

VI

If they knew [he thought] how dreadfully indifferent it all is. How little it matters to me deep down how little I care about it. I'm not interested in how it will go on it will go on anyway. How long [he thought] I didn't see it and yet it went on and the only things I've retained are a few dark patches and a few bright ones and if one hadn't practised again that there are such things one wouldn't know that there are such things. All this [he thought] has come together in me is not together anywhere else a collection of something and something else. Here and there something shifts to one side turns about is there from the back mingles falls but does not change does not change essentially always remains the same. Perhaps [he thought] it is a lesson. If I stick it out keep it up I shall have finished the course before I've started it. Is the start already the finish and is it easier if one is weaned from it at the same time and is it all over when it's over.

VII
Perhaps with those one has to set up a number of objects. Has to be courteous with them and then not trouble about them. Mix with them and forget them. Hide them completely and say everything about them. For it seems they exist only from the outside. Only what comes out exists. Are they hollow inside? Hollow and the hollow filled with something? Tubes of toothpaste? The whole a procedure by which one squeezes out the filling inside? He was still disappointed. What comes out. Comes out in unbroken seeming. Fixed. Or variants of fiction. Motions stirrings pilings incisions expulsions spasms curves distortions knots gleam. Something one has to learn learn by heart and learnt by heart invent forget and rediscover?

VIII
Dedicated to Hans W. Pump who died on July 7 1957 at Esmarkholm while playing badminton.

NOVEL

I
I am a story.

II
I am a story about somebody.

III
Somebody about whom I am a story is the story that I am. I am somebody who is a story.

IV
I don't narrate. I am narrated. As I am being narrated that which is to be narrated narrates itself.

V
Narrated. Not repeated.

VI
Butterfly and Crosscurrent and I Want to be Happy and Night and Day.

VII
The story is a story that happens. A story that at all times has already happened. That will happen and does not cease to happen.

VIII
A story that has ended is not a story. A story that hasn't yet begun has not yet begun.

IX
Stars and clock chimes and footfalls and talking voices.

X
It was yesterday. Was it yesterday? Or will it be only tomorrow after all? The day after tomorrow? Or today?

XI
What has happened in the story is the process of the story. The process of the story proceeds.

XII
The process of the story cannot be interrupted. The story is that process which cannot be interrupted.

XIII
I don't know. I forget. I remember. I experience. It is brought home to me.

XIV
Then. Then and then. That and that then and then. Chronological geographical.

XV
I am that which cannot turn back. The story is that which cannot turn back.

XVI
A propos of something. In consequence of something.

XVII
Consequences of consequences of consequences of consequences of consequences.

XVIII
I am somebody who is the sole true and real story. I am the sole true and real story *about* somebody.

XIX
Truth and reality of the story that I am are that story.

XX
There.

XXI
Irreversibly there.

TREATISE

This is the kind of thing inside which I am and I don't know what kind of thing it is but I know that I've always known that it is a kind of thing of which I don't know what kind of thing it is. But even if I knew what kind of thing it is inside which I am and what it looks like the thing I am inside I should still be inside that kind of thing and not know how to get out and it wouldn't be of any use. Sometimes when I'm doing my bit and doing my bit is that which I can do and doing my bit is that which I know about the thing I am inside I think of it and what I think of is that I am inside and what occurs to me is that it ceases and I don't know what it is that occurs to me when it occurs to me that I shall cease being inside and what that will look like when I shall have ceased being inside it. And when I think that I shall cease to be inside it and what it looks like when I shall have ceased to be inside it and I don't know what it looks like and I can't think of anything else [to think what kind of thing it is when I shall have ceased to be inside that kind of thing inside which I am] then it happens.

If the kind of thing inside which I am had ceased and I could speak and tell and say so and so and this thing inside which I was is that and that and begins here and ceases there and when it has ceased it is only the thing I am no longer inside of any old thing a so and so. But I don't know and it happens.

What happens is what happens when happening ceases. When that happens which happens in the end and again and again. When that happens which causes the thinking of it to cease [and thinking what kind of thing it is inside which I am ceases and thinking what it is when I shall have ceased to be inside it is ceasing to think what it is and yet not ceasing to be inside it and that kind of thing not ceasing to be that kind of thing].

To think what it is to have ceased to be inside it and not to be able to think that I shall have ceased to be inside it this thinking is ceasing to think and this kind of ceasing to think is not a ceasing to remember it. And this ceasing to think and not ceasing to remember is the kind of thing inside which I am. This mesh of the kind of thing I am inside.

SITUATION

Without memory standing in total darkness. The floor damp smooth slippery. When one bends forward one feels the coldness of the floor as of stone or steel. One can move ahead only slowly. When one moves ahead one feels that the floor consists of large irregular slabs separated by narrow but deep grooves.

Assuming one moves ahead. Assuming the only thing one is carrying is a box of matches with let us say ten matches in it. When one lights one of these matches one sees no more than the small vault in the darkness that this feeble light is able to fill. One doesn't even see exactly what the floor is really like. If one is willing to move ahead one lights a second match. Lighting match after match will one slide forward over the slippery floor. Forward? Does one know it is forward?

Assuming one gets somewhere. Assuming one collides with something and assuming one still has one or two matches [it won't be more in any event] one will now spend them without hesitation even with a certain recklessness. When one will have lit the last match one will see a prop at best or [perhaps and in the extreme case] a row of props.

No one will manage to reach the end of the row of props by the light of one match. But the legend has it that one or another [or only one person once] blindly crawling did reach the end. But what one has to imagine is the absolute end beyond this provisional end of the row of props. That is when one has got that far one will get a little [more or less far that no longer makes any difference there] farther. Then the floor will be at an end and whoever has crawled or slid that far will feel the no less smooth and cold vertical beneath him.

At full length perhaps he will then be lying on the verge of the chasm his head extended into the void. He listens. And when he listens he will hear a noise far off that swells and fades out. But this noise will be full of attraction. Not so much that one wants to hurl oneself down. Yet so much that one is held fast there. And if perhaps [and in the extreme case] even at this point one has senselessly not given up the foolish hope that it will be light again one forgets it here. And the only thing one is likely to think is that it's coming closer.

THE MOST CONSIDERATE PERSON IN THE WORLD

I
When he was a child he had a fondness for stories with a happy ending. And still has a fondness for stories with a happy ending. Is startled on his left foot. Is forgetful. Forgets his own birthday for instance. Is sometimes struck by the strangeness of the most everyday things [rain a window his own hand]. Has forgotten that there are such things [rain a window his own hand]. Has good taste. Can't imagine other people having good taste. Is in the habit of saying: when I visit people I stay until I have said everything [and a bit longer at times]. Always feels inclined to stay a bit longer. The clothes he wears adapt themselves to him. Become comfortable [not elegant not correct]. Is all of a piece. Is all of a piece because he doesn't care. Because he forgets to care.

II
Doesn't know what impression he makes. Doesn't know what he looks like. Sees his reflection in the mirror. Is startled by his reflection in the mirror. Occasionally realizes that his effect is such and such. Sums up those realizations. Has no image. [At times it occurs to him that the same thing happened once before. Remembers that at that time he must have had such and such an appearance. Suddenly sees the image of the person he must have been at that time. Recognizes it quite clearly. Sees himself at that time. Does not see himself now.]

III
Speaks without reservations. Enters completely into a conversation. Without making much of it. As a speaker is the reverse side of his speaking. Is the reverse side all round as it were [dumbly]. Forgets his interlocutor as soon as he is alone. Just hangs him up somewhere. Keeps him somewhere. But doesn't give him a thought.

IV

Doesn't [when he thinks of someone] think of the person. The person presents himself to him by general aspects. As a pattern as part of a pattern. As an occasion. In any case thinks [when he thinks] in wholly general terms always. In guide lines in complexes in relationships. Likens connects orders combines creates perspectives for himself. Or lets himself go. Drifts from hypothesis to hypothesis. Penetrates. Astonished without being surprised. Perceives without having imagined. Has no pre-suppositions.

V

Has sometimes thought that he would never have certain experiences. That his whole life would be over without his having had this and that experience. Then says [later] I have learnt from experience. Altogether I have learnt from experience. This one experience [which I haven't had] wouldn't look any different from the experiences I have had. There is nothing besides. What I experience is what I can experience. [At bottom] believes that experience is bad experience. [At the same time] believes that there is no such thing as a bad experience. Is convinced of the rightness of experience.

VI

When something happens doesn't know what will come of it. After the event has always known what will come of it. Is not surprised. Pretends that he is not surprised. [When confronted with something that unwinds] advocates the doctrine of the tangled ball of thread. Everything will always become more tangled if one is violent and has no patience. Everything will straighten itself out if one follows the thread patiently. Believes that he knows just this or that fortuitous thread. Observes without being able to express. Points and lines without connection. Is convinced that there is such a thing as uninhibited connection so to speak. Recognizes connection by looking.

VII
Must make use of time in which he has time. Must look out for opportunity in which he has opportunity. Puzzle games that have nothing to do but wait for him. For him who does not decide but is decided.

VIII
He has understanding. But he does not use it for doing. He uses it for talking about things.

GRAMMATICAL REDUCTION

If I were not only I but we I should be you he she it. Since I am I and not we I am I and can speak only of me. If I were we I should be speaking of us when I am speaking of me. Because I am I and can speak only of me I do not speak of us. But I think while I am speaking of me [as though we]. I speak as though I were we. [We should be we if we could speak of us. We has no speech. We is a phantom made up of I plus I plus I. This phantom of I plus I plus I is a phantom because we cannot speak of us.]
You speak when you speak of you as he who [I] speaks of himself. He she it speaks as the one who [I] speaks of himself herself itself. You don't exist because I cannot speak of you. He she it doesn't exist because I cannot speak of him her it. And so forth. You is an idea of mine. He she it are ideas of mine. [If I were you if I were he she it I could speak of you all and of them all.]
When I speak of me as of me I speak of me with the help of a grammatical fiction. If I speak of you speak of him speak of us speak of all of you I speak with the help of a grammatical fiction. Of what I speak I speak with the help of. If I am I because I can speak of me I can speak of me only with the help of. If I can speak of me as of thee him us you only with the help of I too am an idea of mine. If I is an idea of mine I don't exist. I don't exist because when I speak of me I can do so only with the help of. But I am no phantom. For the idea of me is an idea of mine.
I exist [everything of which I can speak exists] because I step out of this circle [with the help of] and go beyond the fiction and speak as though not. I speak as though not because the speech that I speak speaks as though.
I speak when I speak in a language that is strange to my speech. To my speech the language in which I speak is inappropriate. Speaking in the language that has grown strange to the speech this language becomes different. Speaking in the language that its speech makes for itself the speech makes the speaker's language a different language. Which ceases to be strange to his speech.

POLITICAL GRAMMAR

Persecutors persecute the persecuted. But the persecuted become persecutors. And because the persecuted become persecutors the persecuted become persecuting persecuted and persecutors become persecuted persecutors. Persecuted persecutors however in their turn become persecutors [persecuting persecuted persecutors]. And the persecuting persecuted in their turn become persecuted [persecuted persecuting persecuted]. Turn the persecutors into persecuted. Turn the persecuting persecuted into persecuted persecutors. Turn the persecuting persecuted persecutors into persecuted persecuting persecuted. And so ad infinitum.

Neither the persecuted nor the non-persecuted persecute neither the persecutors nor the persecuted. Are neither persecutors nor non-persecutors of persecutors as of persecuted. Neither persecuted nor non-persecuted outside the grammatical circle persecute persecution. Persecute persecution in persecutors as in persecuted. In persecuted persecutors as in persecuting persecuted. In persecuting persecuted persecutors as in persecuted persecuting persecuted. In persecuting persecution they also persecute non-persecution [the non-persecution of persecution]. In that case neither the persecuted nor the non-persecuted would be the true persecutors.

As persecutors of persecution in persecutors as in non-persecutors they are persecuted by persecutors as by the persecuted. As persecutors of the non-persecution of persecution they are persecuted by non-persecutors as by the non-persecuted. Persecutors of persecution and of non-persecution they would be the ones truly persecuted. Not the persecuting persecuted and the persecuted persecutors. But persecutors and persecuted at the same time.

FROM *GENERALIZATION*

WEDDING RECEPTION

someone sees someone standing next to something and looking at something and stops himself.
someone sees someone stopping and looking at someone who is standing next to something and looking at something and stops himself
someone plus someone [plus someone] those are people who stop and look at someone who is standing next to something and looking at something
some people stop looking at some who stop and look at someone who is standing next to something and looking at something [stop because someone has seen someone who was standing next to something and looking at something and had stopped himself]
in the end some people are simply standing around someone who is standing next to something and looking at something
Someone who is standing next to something and looking at something
someone who is standing next to something and looking at something suddenly ceases to look at it and looks at these people who
someone looks at those who have stopped because someone has looked at him standing next to something and looking at something and in his turn had stopped
someone looks at these people and doesn't know why they stopped
someone looks at those who are looking at him and is startled and walks on
those who saw him standing next to something look at the thing he looked at now look at someone who is looking at them and is startled and walks on those who look at him walking on don't know what he was looking at and they only look at someone who is startled and walks on
and because they look at nothing but someone who is startled and walks on and because they don't know why they look at one another and as they look at one another they see by the other's look that no one knew and they disperse and walk on
but everyone who walks on looks back and sees everyone who is walking on look back and everyone who walks on and sees everyone walking on looking back now bewares of stopping

BLACKCURRANTS

someone goes there and does something
someone goes there and does it because where he goes he finds something that can be done and finds it because that which can be done and what he does is something that is where he goes and does something
that which someone does where he goes is not anything any more than someone is anyone or somewhere anywhere but that which someone does when he goes there where he goes is something quite special for where he goes what he does is something he can do only there and i.e. this thing to which he goes is something that can not only be done but one that makes him do something i.e. that which he does at the same time is something that makes him do and doing and making someone do are bound up in this connection
but where he goes to do something and be made to do something someone else can go too and do and be made to do and so a third fourth etc. and for all who go there this thing they go to is something that makes them do what they do
and so one can say many go where there is something that makes them do what they do and in that they go there where there is something that makes them do what they do many are alike
they are alike because this thing to which they go because it makes them do something is also something they do and because making someone do something and doing are the same thing where they go and because they are the same thing the likeness between them because of it for the moment is the only likeness between them i.e. this fact that they go where there is something that makes them do what they do is the standard by which they are comparable
for a person who simply and literally only wanted to do any old thing could also literally go anywhere and not just where something makes him do what he does but that he does so indeed that he evidently has no idea of not doing it means that he belongs with all those others who have no other idea and so it turns out at last that the thing that brings them together where they go is something which leaves them with no other idea and that that which makes them comparable is just that they have no other idea
but since they have no other idea they have no other choice either and

since they have no other choice they don't like anyone else to have a choice either and so from the start their ambition is that where they go everyone shall go for only when all go there and become comparable one can discover what is at stake where they all go [for what is at stake is that all go where there is something that makes all of them do what all of them do]

TOURIST SEASON

but despite all that woe to those who want to hinder journeys as long as they are necessary
Ludwig Hohl

district is something in which something happens and in which something comes together to which something is happening district is something with something there and in a way it is formed by what is there and which comes together and happens in a way consists entirely of what is there and all that is there is there only because it occurs in that district and being there in a way means from the start that it occurs there and district and being there are things which so to speak only occur together and are hard to keep separate and are interchangeable so to speak.
landscape is something one approaches that one enters in which one finds oneself and finding oneself finds good or bad as one finds it landscape is also something one simply finds finds beautiful finds ugly finds boring finds magnificent landscape is also something for which one feels something something that one enjoys and admires and admiring envisages places oneself in front of
now a strange habit makes one aspire away from districts to landscapes and repeat that performance year after year or all the time and there seem to be times when this urge is stronger and others when it is weaker indeed one could divide all times into districts and landscapes nobody wants to spend his holidays in a district and if district is something in which being there is the only thing so to speak that occurs landscapes of course are the only escape district is that where one is anyway and landscape is something that gives scope for envisaging
although of course it happens again and again that those who are there anyway can't understand at all why the others go there and those and the others agree that that and the other must be destroyed only no one has yet discovered which they really want to destroy districts or landscapes

FROM *3 x 13 MORE-OR-LESS STORIES*

SCHEMATIC DEVELOPMENT OF TRADITION

those who were not there were more numerous than those who were there always those who are not there are more numerous than those who are there
so those who were there thought of those who were not there and so always those who are there think of those who are not there and all that those who are there do and resolve to do occurs in memory of those who are not there
did those who were not there also think of those who were there
those who were there did not know those who are there do not know and those who will be there will not know those who are there do not know whether one can speak of memory with regard to those who are not there those who were not there were there at one time
even when they had been there too those who had not been there had been more numerous than those who had been there those who had been there had been fewer than those who had not been there as long as those who had been there could remember
but if those who were not there have always been more numerous than those who were there and if always fewer have been there than were not there and if all that those who have been there are there and will be there do and resolve to do occurs in memory of those who are not there then those who are there are always only there in the name of those who are not there only in the name of those who were not there those who were there were really there
to be really there means to be there in the name of those who are not there means to be there in the name of those who are more numerous and always would be more numerous immeasurably more to be there no longer and be more numerous means the criterion for being there to have been there is that which determines always has determined and always will determine being there
and those who had been there became those who were no longer there and those who are there will become those who will no longer be there and of that which they did or resolved to do in memory of those who were not there they took something with them and of that which they now do or resolve to do in memory of those who are no longer there they will have taken something with them when they will no longer be there and so those who are no longer there have already taken with

them an immeasurable amount of that which those who were there did and resolved to do in memory of those who were not there an immeasurable amount is in the possession of those who are not there and it will continue to be more the fact that they have it in their possession and that this possession continues to grow is that which in regard to those who are not there one could call the memory of those who are there

because those who are no longer there have once been there

not to be there is something of which one thinks in being there and to be there is consumption of the possession still being accumulated by those who are not there

in the name of those who are no longer there and are more numerous because those who are no longer there and are more numerous have a name and we are there in that name

SOCIAL CONTRACT

one is with another and assuming they are the only ones that exist the one is like this and the other is not like this either the one becomes half not like this and the other becomes half like this or they try to separate or the one kills the other or the other kills the one and the matter is settled

but now there are three and still assuming they are the only ones that exist the one is like this the second also the third is not like this or the one is like this the second and third are not like this etc. then either one becomes half like this and the other two half not like this or vice versa or all of them become neither like this nor not like this etc. or they try to separate or two kill the third or one kills the other two and at once the matter is settled

but now there are four or five or fifty or a thousand or a hundred thousand or a million or two billions and a half and each is different from the other many of them not very different but all a bit many too are a bit alike of course and because again and again there are a few a bit alike they get on all right and there isn't violence and murder all the time till there is no one left but those who get on because of one bit of likeness between them are now a bit more different from those who get on because of another bit of likeness between them

and if now they don't find something a bit alike in those others things go wrong and there are violence and murder attack and defence blitz-krieg chain bombing invasion and capitulation and still the matter is not settled

but now at last many more who are a bit alike and get on find a bit of likeness in the many others who are a bit alike and many others again find many others again and now on the one hand there are these first many more who are a bit alike and then a bit of a bit more and finally still a bit of a bit more and get on and on the other hand there are those other many more who are a bit alike in another way and then another bit of a bit more and finally still another bit of a bit more and get on and assuming they are the only ones that exist two billions and a half at a rough estimate they now form two blocks and cannot get on even if all of them

FINAL SOLUTION

they just happened to think that up one day
who happened to think that up one day
that just happened to occur to them
to whom did that just happen to occur
to one of them that just happened to occur
one of them just happened to think that up one day
one of them just happened to just think that up one day
or perhaps more than one of them thought it up at the same time
perhaps that occurred to more than one of them together
and how did they carry out the thing that occurred to them

if one wants to get anything done one has to be for something and not just something one happens to think up but something for which one can be or at least something for which a lot of people would like to be or at least something one imagines a lot of people would like to be for
and they just happened to think that up one day
they thought that up and then they hit on the idea when they wanted to start doing something but what they hit on was not something one can be for but something one can be against or better something one can bring most people round to being against for when one can bring most people round to being against something one needn't be so precise any more about the thing one can be for and the fact that one needn't be so precise about it any more has its advantages for if most people can just let themselves go they usually don't care what it is they are for
and so they hit on that idea when they'd started to just think up something of the kind
so they hit on the idea that what one is against must be something one can see touch revile humiliate spit at lock up strike down annihilate because what one can't see touch revile humiliate spit at lock up strike down annihilate one can only speak of and what one can only speak of can change and one never quite knows what it will turn into whatever one may say against it
and so they hit on that idea and did that
so they hit on that idea and did that and when they had done that they

tried to bring most people round and when they had brought most people round to joining in they hit on the idea that what one is against so long as it's still there remains changeable and that only what's gone becomes unchangeable and so they forced those they had brought round to joining in to annihilate that which they had been brought round to being against to regard it like malaria mosquitoes or chickweed or wireworm that have to be exterminated and when they had managed that they called those they had brought round to doing that murderers and turned them too into malaria mosquitoes and chickweed and wireworm and kept them down as they had wanted to keep them down without being for anything but just to keep them down for ever

and that just happened to occur to them when they hit on the idea that one can do all those things

that just happened to occur to them when they wanted to do something and then they hit on the idea that all one needs is to bring some people round to being for something at first and to being against something and so on until they can't get out of it any more and run round in circles for all eternity or rather till there is no one left for that won't take them till all eternity

but why did they think that up or didn't they think anything of it except that they wanted to do something perhaps because it was too boring for them as it was before that occurred to them and they hit on the idea

yes of course they carried it so far only so that in the end they themselves could plunge into it and put an end to themselves and to everything for people like that are always people who want to put an end to it but they don't want to go by themselves but everyone must go with them

so that's the kind of people to whom something like that just happens to occur

CATALOGUE OF THE INCORRIGIBLE

there are incorrigible people who think that everything will be the same again
there are incorrigible people who know that nothing will be the same again but who behave as though it will be
there are incorrigible people who know that nothing will be the same again they behave as though it will be and try to pass on the tale
there are incorrigible people who know that nothing will be the same again and they don't behave as though it will be but they haven't understood how things are
there are incorrigible people who have understood how things are but they believe that everything will be the same again and that they'll bring it off again one day
there are incorrigible people who have understood how things are and think they have understood that it will be the same again if not quite as it was the first time
there are incorrigible people who have understood how things are but they don't believe in what they have understood and think that things are always changing
there are incorrigible people who know that nothing will be the same again and have understood how things are and still can't give up and try once more
there are incorrigible people who know that nothing will be the same again and have understood how things are and still can't give up and theorize about it
there are incorrigible people who act as though nothing happened and live in splendour and joy
there are incorrigible people who act as though nothing happened and have understood how things are and do again what they please
there are incorrigible people who act as though nothing happened and have understood how things are and know that it will never be the same again and do again what they please
incorrigible survivors

SHORT STORY

she had something going with her she had something going with him
what did he have going with her what did she have going with him
he also had something going with him there she also had something going with her there
what did he also have going with him there what did she also have going with her there
he had something going with her and also with him there
what did he have going with her and also with him there
she had something going with him and also with her there
what did she have going with him and also with her there

he had something going with himself she had something going with herself
what did he have going with himself what did she have going with herself

he had it did he have it she had it did she have it

he had something going with her and also with him there and with himself she had something going with him and also with her there and with herself he had something going with her and also with him there and with himself and even with her there she had something going with him and also with her there and with herself and even with him there he there had something going with him and her and her there she there had something going with her and him and him there did he there also have something going with himself did she there also have something going with herself

A SIMPLE STORY

he had been her
she had been his
she had had him for
they had gone together
they had gone out together
they had gone to bed together
they had been together a
all this happened long ago

for her another also had a
but she had not had one for anyone else
but the other had not ceased to
so he had become her other
but she had still not had one for anyone else
that hadn't mattered to him
so he had remained her other
it had done him no good nor her
and this too happened long ago

then she lost the one who had been her
she had no one now
it was a great
that made her very
she had a really hard
that completely
no one else could be to her what
that completely and she simply couldn't
but this too happened long ago

all this happened long ago
she now has someone else for
it is the other who had not ceased to
he still has not ceased to
he is her
he is with her
he doesn't want anything but what he now
although he hadn't been her
but that to him is no
although at times for him with her it isn't quite

she wonders how it would be if the one at that time hadn't
she wonders how it would be if the one of that time were again to
would he be her if he were again to she wonders
would she be his if he were again to she wonders
would they together again if he were again to she wonders
would everything she wonders begin again just
would they she wonders begin again just and no differently if
they again

couldn't she have would have been simpler still
she would have had the one and the other
she would have been both the one's and the other's
one of them would have vanished emigrated fallen died
would have left her sued her been sued done a bunk
the other would have and wouldn't have any of those things
she would simply have remained only his and he her
would have remained
wouldn't be wondering if
would have been not and not
would have been not and not and would be still

FAMILY POLITICS

Adam marries Betty Betty marries Caesar Caesar marries Dorette Dorette marries Edward Edward marries Sheila Sheila marries Gerald Gerald marries Harriet Harriet marries Jacob Jacob marries Cordula Cordula marries Adam

Adam not only marries Betty and is taken in marriage by Cordula he also marries and is taken in marriage by Caesar Dorette Edward Sheila Gerald Harriet Jacob in the same way Betty not only marries Caesar and is taken in marriage by Adam she also marries and is taken in marriage by Dorette Edward Sheila Gerald Harriet Jacob Cordula and so on down the line

Adam Betty Caesar Dorette Edward Sheila Gerald Harriet Jacob and Cordula are inter-married and form a family because they are inter-married and together form a single family all relations between them are legitimized and authorized that is insofar as these relations are heterosexual each man can have children with each woman or each woman with each man insofar as they are homosexual no criminal act takes place

Adam enters into a relationship with Betty Caesar enters into a relationship with Dorette Edward enters into a relationship with Sheila Gerald enters into a relationship with Harriet Jacob enters into a relationship with Cordula or Adam enters into a relationship with Caesar Betty enters into a relationship with Dorette Edward enters into a relationship with Gerald Sheila enters into a relationship with Harriet Jacob enters into a relationship with Adam Cordula enters into a relationship with Betty or Adam enters into relationships with Betty and Dorette Caesar enters into relationships with Sheila and Harriet Edward enters into relationships with Cordula and Betty Gerald enters into relationships with Dorette and Sheila Jacob enters into relationships with Harriet and Cordula or Betty enters into relationships with Adam and Dorette Sheila enters into relationships with Caesar and Harriet Cordula enters into relationships with Edward and Betty Dorette enters into relationships with Gerald and Sheila Harriet enters into relationships with Jacob and Cordula

certain bounds are set by the circumstances that not at all times each man can maintain a relationship with each woman or each man with each man or each woman with each man or each woman with each woman but that is only a question of practical management that does not affect the principle far less invalidates it

Adam fathers a child with Betty Caesar fathers a child with Dorette Edward fathers a child with Sheila Gerald fathers a child with Harriet Jacob fathers a child with Cordula Cordula has a child by Adam Betty has a child by Caesar Dorette has a child by Edward Sheila has a child by Gerald Harriet has a child by Jacob

Adam's children are Betty's children Caesar's children are Dorette's children Edward's children are Sheila's children Gerald's children are Harriet's children Jacob's children are Cordula's children but Betty's children are also Caesar's Dorette's Edward's Sheila's Gerald's Harriet's Jacob's Cordula's children and so on down the line

certain bounds are set to procreation of course by the circumstance that in the case of general heterosexual relations no children can be conceived the function of the family association true would not be disturbed by that since under the complete legitimization of all relations within the family this would constitute only one instance

it should be added that this is a model that can be enlarged varied and complicated ad lib. and in any way you like

BREMEN WHEREYOU

whereyou
what
whereyou
what
whereyouwere
where
youwere
inBremenofcourse
andhe
andwho
washe
washewhat
washethere
inBremen
washethereinBremen
yeshewasthereinBremen
andshe
andwho
wasshethere
shewastheretoo
shewastheretooinBremen
yesshewastheretooinBremen

andthere
andtherewhat
andthereyouwerealltogether
inBremen
andthereyouwerealltogetherinBremen
yesofcourse
inBremen
yesofcoursewewerealltogetherinBremen
andthereyoudid
therewedidwhat
didyoudothatthingImean
didwedothatthingyoumean
didyoudothatthingaltogetherImean

didwedothatthingalltogetheryoumean
didyoudothatthingalltogetherinBremen
don'tyouknowthat
don'tIknowwhat
thatwedidthatthing
thatyoudidthatthing
yesthatwedidthatthingalltogether
alltogether
yeswediditalltogether
inBremen
yeswedidthatthingalltogetherinBremen

andwithChristmassonear

BAD NEWS

a certain Mr Job or whatever he was a sort of successful man he had influence like and power like a sort of Mr Lucky you might say or whatever Leviathan and Behemoth or whatever at his service for he was afraid he was afraid and fear was all he had he possessed it and it possessed him and whenever he was a sort of successful man it was because he was afraid

as he grew older he was succceeded by his son Job Junior he too was a sort of successful man but without fear because fear was not an inheritance like but something one either had or didn't have

the success of Job Junior increased and there was a moment when it was greater than Job Senior's and at that very moment perhaps only at that moment when Job Junior's success was greater than Job Senior's Job lost his fear and when he looked for it the next moment it was too late he couldn't find it again it was lost

and as he lost it he lost his son in the midst of his growing success and as he lost his son he lost his success his influence his power relatives disowned him people well disposed to him proved to be envious friends to be sycophants authorities to be enemies what was left his creditors mortgaged

so he tried Mr Unlucky or whatever to find his fear again he set out to look for it in this country and that wherever he could hope to find something like fear but he didn't find it instead of being afraid he felt enterprising he was going down in the end he's sitting there this Mr Job or whatever a man at the end of his fifties in a motorcar like at the side of a motorway like in a deserted area like where other successful people like rush past him in other motorcars like

didn't I think he says that I've always had enough of this fear that I can't find again now O my son Jonathan who has stolen my fear without which I can't you might say live instead I'm full of exuberance very soon one of those passing by in a hurry will come to me and all will be well

but those passing by in a hurry as you might call them kept their eyes like fixed right in front of them in a manner of speaking night is falling Mr Job or whatever goes off into the countryside he finds woods as it were and fallow land he comes to a house like and goes in the floor is rotten it breaks under him he lies there and can't get up again feels pain and hunger and thirst he cries out no one hears him may-be wind like or light like and shadow and Behemoth and Leviathan dead long ago

his attempt to feel something like fear weakens he is content not to find fear again light and shadow alternate faster and when was it anyway asks Job or whatever when I was mistaken for that which I owned like with sisterly brotherly brotherinlawly bonds now is is directed at that which I am beginning to gain and I am content it is like a great unsistering unbrothering unbrotherinlawing removing untwining to have ceased is like being like being away

slowly and painfully it ends bit by bit he is content according to

THE QUESTION OF IDENTITY

between
Auschwitz
and
Alabama
if
I
knew
that
it
is
I
left
over
where
to
be
left
over
have-been
for
no
one
indifferent
how
candidly
I
talk
of
myself
victim
tautology
of the century
speechless
beyond grammar
the horizon of operations
infinite

nil
the
fear
of
the
century
sunk
like
jobs
to
be
found
whether
prosperity
lasts
war
avoidable
bashed into a fine point
that
our visible world
the
last
that
proportions of the not to be rationalized
without
expansion
inaudible
screaming
if
that
is
the
end
I
am
finite

EXPLANATION OF THE RHINOCEROS

I

if as the idiom has it to be pigeon-toed and sit behind the window and observe people are a sign of character he had character if to live behind the moon and to leave well alone detracts from character he had no or little character yet he was a good walker often on the move at all corners and ends often if one looked closely he was already gone with gusto but a bit morose that is externally for he was afraid he might lose his zest if he wore it openly on his face

II

his arguments were of this kind the rhino is called the rhino because it is a rhinoceros and speaks Latin human beings can be rhinoceroces too but pedagogues know everything because someone who teaches others can't be taught himself silence has nothing to do with pedagogy humanity can be divided into rhinoceroses and non-rhinoceroses [pedagogues were the people he liked least]

III

for a time he collected what he called the devotional dialect those considerations in which it can be a merit to have demonstrated something unobtrusively [an especially rare example] after respectful thinking-it-so [a turn of phrase no longer current] inclined to come to speak of it in my own person belated execution closer to the case with immediately staggering spontaneity [immediate staggering] instrumented energy quiet creative power that originates at the beginning the attestation arising from intensification in an almost bold and sinister venture

IV

he invented proverbs like one has the best of it one is best at it one knows best but the one who knows best is not best at it the one who is best at it doesn't have the best of it one gets the worst one draws a blank and one does tomorrow what he could do today but the one who does tomorrow what he could do today doesn't draw a blank doesn't get the worst he invented titles like Max the faun wears long underpants or beau Beau

V

he told stories like this one that the reason why the negotiations over this matter broke down had nothing to do with the matter nor with the attitudes of the negotiators to the matter but only with the various relations between the figures

VI

he was a lover of every kind of picture book [he was also a proverbial reader one could not imagine him in the act of not reading] he predicted the dissolution of primers and textbooks into picture books and proclaimed the imminent approach of this dissolution as a turning-point in his dreams he anticipated such books and described those dreams as the pure manifestation of utopia

VII

he owned a collection of pocket watches one of which he always carried on him and all of which he was in the habit of winding up in turn [irregularly] but he hardly ever used them but relied on broadcast announcements railway station clocks church clocks shadows constellations or simply on his sense of time he was always astonished to find that his watches when he did happen to glance at them seemed to keep more or less correct time so much outside himself

VIII

the axiom that one turns to numbers when one is beginning to lose one's perspective everyone thinks he is lost as soon as he loses his perspective hence statistics but who remembers how wonderful it is to have lost one's perspective all the things that emerge then but of course [he always said] and that's an attraction it's far more exciting still to lose one's perspective in statistics though a bit abstract

IX

the strange state in which one finds oneself when one regards everything one likes to remember as noteworthy and worth communicating but [he always said] what would literature be without that and the only bad thing is to be in that state and unable to do it any more

X
the future to him was something of greater or lesser volume of almost indefinite extension on some days compressible as though into one hand on others surveyable and unsurveyable his only constant fear that it could be only too surveyable the past on the other hand appeared to him as something that constantly adds itself up as it were while the space available for it always remains the same but the individual marks always that much smaller because they all fit into that space but the past was also something that always attaches visibly audibly smellably tastably feelably readably to everything that one sees hears smells tastes feels and reads something that in any case doesn't simply exist in its own right but only in relation to what is there [and history really only in the form of stories]

XI
that it's wrenched out of one's hand if one holds on to it that one always only wants to hold on to that which will be wrenched out of one's hand fear at the alarm bells of ambulances immediately bound up with the superstition that ambulances bring you luck if you see them pass in the morning to be sure hearses are safer

XII
characteristically there are no descriptions of him not even pictures instead there is the place in the hotel lounge where he ate fruit the window behind which he'd fallen asleep with his forehead pressed to the panes till a boy from the outside woke him in a village the rock on which he slipped and fell into the snow at one of his hosts' the tabletop on which his hands got into fights with objects over such places he gradually distributed himself until he had vanished [to want to vanish like that publisher's traveller at Allingham who one morning leapt into the air a bit in the sun opposite a newspaper kiosk and was gone]

XIII
although as the idiom has it he has now vanished for good he is not gone rather it is as though he had merely chosen a still more

voluminous body in which grown-up people walk with children through the afternoon sunshine down a path in the park [many paths in many parks in many cities] old men sit on benches trams are steered into bends on a higher level suburban trains hesitantly pull out of stations smoke trails of steamers cross horizons the slanted cut of the valley behind Ronco is blurred by rainclouds or the straight line formed by the flat wall behind the colonnades of the harbour in Genoa means the temporary end of the world

XIV
in memory of Ferdinand Lion

CLASS ANALYSIS

a thingumy [stuffed shirt bourgeois member of the property-owning class monopoly capitalist] who regards a thingumy [stuffed shirt bourgeois member of the property-owning class monopoly capitalist] as a thingumy [stuffed shirt bourgeois member of the property-owning class monopoly capitalist] does not regard him as a thingumy [stuffed shirt bourgeois member of the property-owning class monopoly capitalist] but as something better

for that sort of thingumy is a thingumy and a thingumy who is a thingumy sees nothing in a thingumy but the thingumy and not himself and because in the thingumy he sees the thingumy that he is himself but not himself he sees something better in the thingumy for a thingumy who is a thingumy is like that and as for his thingumybobness he never even notices that it is a thingumybobness of that kind and because he is like that and never notices it he regards his thingumybobness as something better

a thingumy of that kind is conditioned by his regarding every thingumybobness as something better his thingumybobness is conditioned by his seeing not himself in the thingumy that he is but something better and this conditioning makes him determined to rise above himself he fulfils his conditions in that his conditioning leads not to self-knowledge but to something better and if he really regarded a thingumy as a thingumy and saw himself in that thingumy he would regard it as something worse for assuming that a thingumy regarded a thingumy only as a thingumy and not as something better but saw himself in it as something worse as something he did not want to regard himself as he would be forced to regard a thingumy as something neither better nor worse but simply as that sort of thingumy and that would really amount to self-knowledge

but that's what he does not do that's the very thing he clearly does not do and just because he clearly does not do it he is just as clearly conditioned

and so the thingumy remains a thingumy (stuffed shirt bourgeois member of the property-owning class monopoly capitalist) and regards all thingumybobs (stuffed shirts bourgeois members of the property-owning class monopoly capitalists) not as thingumybobs (stuffed shirts bourgeois members of the property-owning class monopoly capitalists) but as something better and does not change

THE NEW AGE

when who meets whom and what he says when he meets whom and then he says what when he calls whom what
when a cold warrior meets a cold warrior and says cold warrior when a fellow traveller meets a fellow traveller and says fellow traveller when an ex-Nazi calls an ex-Nazi an ex-Nazi
when an intellectual calls an intellectual an ex-Nazi when an avant-gardist meets an avant-gardist and says cold warrior when a non-conformist meets a non-conformist and says fellow traveller
when a fellow traveller meets a fellow traveller and says hippie
and when an ex-Nazi calls an ex-Nazi an experimentalist and when a cold warrior meets a cold warrior and says homosexual swine
when an intellectual meets an ex-Nazi and says homosexual swine when an avant-gardist calls a cold warrior an experimentalist when a non-conformist meets a fellow traveller and says hippie
when a hippie meets a hippie and says ex-Nazi when an experimentalist meets an experimentalist and says fellow traveller when a homosexual swine calls a homosexual swine an intellectual
when he calls him that when he meets him and then says that when he meets him and then says that
all of them join the Communist Party and live happily ever after

THE FUTURE OF SOCIALISM

no one owns anything
no one exploits
no one oppresses
no one is exploited
no one is oppressed
no one gains anything
no one loses anything
no one is a master
no one is a slave
no one is a superior
no one is a subordinate
no one owes anyone anything
no one does anything to anyone

no one owns nothing
no one exploits no one
no one oppresses no one
no one is exploited by no one
no one is oppressed by no one
no one gains nothing
no one loses nothing
no one is no one's master
no one is no one's slave
no one is no one's superior
no one is no one's subordinate
no one owes no one anything
no one does anything to no one

all own everything
all exploit all
all oppress all
all are exploited by all
all are oppressed by all
all gain everything
all lose everything
all are everyone's masters
all are everyone's slaves
all are everyone's superiors
all are everyone's subordinates
all owe everyone everything
all do anything to everyone

all own nothing
all exploit no one
all oppress no one
all are exploited by no one
all are oppressed by no one
all gain nothing
all lose nothing
all are no one's masters
all are no one's slaves
all are no one's superiors
all are no one's subordinates
all owe no one nothing
all do nothing to no one

SO WHAT

the honest people have proved to be corrupt
the decent people have proved to be bogus
vitality proves to be impotence
chastity proves to be oversexed
the sober people have proved to be addicts
the responsible people have proved to be irresponsible
magnanimity proves to be pettiness
discipline proves to be confusion
love of truth has proved to be riddled with lies
fearlessness proves to be cowardice
justice to be cruelty
the life-affirmers prove to be a shifty lot

the corrupt people prove to be the only honest ones
the bogus only are decent people
impotence only is vital
being oversexed is the only kind of chastity
only addiction is sober
only irresponsible people have a sense of responsibility
the petty are the only magnanimous people
confusion alone is disciplined
lies are the only truth
only cowards are fearless
only those who are cruel are just
only those who are a shifty lot are life-affirmers

whoever is honest is corrupt
whoever pretends to be decent is bogus
whoever wants to seem vital produces impotence
whoever wants to seem chaste becomes oversexed
whoever is sober is an addict
whoever wants to take on responsibility is irresponsible
whoever wants to seem magnanimous ought to be petty
whoever believes in discipline is confused
whoever tells the truth is a liar
whoever is fearless is a coward
whoever wants to be just is cruel
whoever affirms life is a shifty lot

honestly corrupt or corruptly honest
decent bogusness or bogus decency
vital impotence or impotent vitality
oversexed chastity or chaste oversexedness
addicted through sobriety or soberly addicted
responsible irresponsibilty or irresponsible responsibility
magnanimously petty or petty magnanimity
disciplined confusion or confused discipline
true lie or truth riddled with lies
fearlessly cowardly or cowardly fearlessness
just cruelty or cruelly just
a shifty lot's affirmation of life or life-affirmingly shifty

so what

THE DILEMMA OF BEING HIGH AND DRY

a man is high and dry and hasn't given up hope of reaching the shore that is the dilemma in which he finds himself but he doesn't like what his relative the water painter does to paint on water

that he is high and dry is a general state of affairs as long as he can't give up this prejudice he is inclined to hallucinate stretches of water in place of stretches of sand water tracks in place of forest tracks wherever he looks he sees mirror surfaces and light and shadow reflections wherever he listens he hears the crying of seagulls and the sound of ships' sirens

he has developed a passion for professions like bargee launch pilot lock-keeper river policeman and lighthouse-keeper and a revulsion towards idioms like you can't build on water to keep one's head above water up to his neck in water a bit close to the water of the first water although he hates making excuses at times looking forward or back he does catch himself arguing as though to excuse himself how it happened to him and others that is to live in a world that one does not see as it is but in goodness knows what fancies

a somewhat self-satisfied man in his mid-forties who sometimes has a rather oppressive effect on other people with a tendency to put on fat not discourteous but thoroughly reserved his eyes mere slits what does a man like that see anyway certainly not the open sea shore landscapes possibly breakwaters landing-stages canal and bridge tracts water the water painter said it must be

FROM *NEW TREATISES ON HUMAN UNDERSTANDING*

A 45-YEAR-OLD ENGLISHWOMAN FROM BIRMINGHAM

reminds him of something that reminds him of something reminds him of something that reminds him a of a girl fields of summer clouds the classical coastline of the clouds cloud contours cloud sails watermarks on the empty noon sky cloud towers of the horizon thunderclouds shadow hands the white clouds of night cloud-white cloud topography on the very first impact peculiar contradictions become evident blue forest noon heat of June peat smell 30 degrees in the shade tar spots in the noon sunshine on the very first impact peculiar contradictions become evident crane cabs rubble overgrown with creepers in the midst of it squadrons of swans the drifting of summer clouds useless conversations capsules rattling one against the other freely moving

wind the whip of the freely moving stroke the paper pressed against the fence symbols of the world of the dead summer rhythms the sudden thunderstorms the lamp patterns of the nights peat smell in July moorland concentration camp in July by now the situation has reached the point again where certain dreams of mine that I remember forgotten dreams brick dust the layering of forests in the rain standing to have fallen down think standing to have fallen down grey cardigan over a Prussian blue pleated skirt memory of heroic Swiss landscape in Wilhelm Meister's Years of Travel or Addrich in the moss peat smell in July moorland concentration camp in July the possibility of confusing Wilhelmshaven in memory with Amsterdam or Paris

because we were looking for sweets for the children green garden table at which one sits used to sit for 6 persons table for 12 persons fit for the table set on the table grey cardigan over a Prussian blue pleated skirt green table garden table table at which one sits used to sit table for 6 persons table for 12 persons fit for the table set on the table the possibility of confusing Wilhelmshaven in memory with Amsterdam or Paris because we were looking for sweets for the children crane cabs layers of the far-reaching landscape colouring of the far-reaching landscape light and shade colours of the far-reaching landscape and many white houses in the green swallows around the tower of clouds wind-motion in the sky memory of heroic Swiss landscape in Wilhelm

Meister's Years of Travel or Addrich in the moss layers of the far-reaching landscape colouring of the far-reaching landscape light and shadow colours of the far-reaching landscape flat polished high scribbled horizon horizontal on the horizon of on the horizon of making some dreams of mine that I remember forgotten dreams brick dust a 45-year-old Englishwoman gave birth in Birmingham to her 22nd child she has been married for 30 years to a welder now 50 fifteen of the children still live with their parents the four eldest daughters have married two children died the father earns £20 a week and has not taken a holiday at any time in his life the layering of forests in rain rainbow-coloured oil patches after thundery rain

orange cleaning trucks of the Stuttgart Tramlines Ltd. Zschocke democraticus June clouds now singing in the June night at that time singing in the June night to be here now means only that one can remember that one can remember it means to be here a hundred and eight-one times moon dream marvel solitude seventy-two times stars fifty-four times bliss the transition consists in that one could demonstrate the wastefulness and so to speak the folly of the capitalist world by the methods of eccentric art in its sceptical relationship to general convention a 45-year-old Englishwoman gave birth in Birmingham to her 22nd child she has been married for 30 years to a welder now 50 fifteen of the children still live with their parents the

four eldest daughters have married two children died the father earns £20 a week and has not taken a holiday at any time in his life movements across the whole sky flat polished high scribbled horizon horizontal on the horizon of on the horizon of making movements across the whole sky one big union man one man big union big man one union big one man union peat smell in July moorland concentration camp in July many white houses in the green swallows around the tower of clouds wind-motion in the sky Zschocke democraticus on a walking-tour to encounter a castle or a ruin is always an enrichment of the day's experience a hundred and eighty-one times moon dream marvel solitude seventy-two times stars fifty-four times bliss lost in a chain of single days green table garden table table at which one sits used to sit table for 6 persons table for 12 persons fit for the table set on the table some dreams of mine that I remember forget dreams the spherical trees of Karl Walser the conical trees of Kate Greenaway standing to have fallen down think standing to have fallen down rainbow-coloured oil patches after thundery rain reddish-blue tints of wet posters satisfaction of the wind on C roads [country lanes] satisfaction of memory on C roads [country lanes] squares of mail delivery vans painted yellow two tram drivers in conversation lost in a chain of single days brick dust on a walking tour to encounter a castle or a ruin is always an enrichment of the day's experience the

pattern of cock-crows in the black valley the distribution of cock-crows in the black valley crossing and variation of cock-crows in the black valley owing to non-observance of the traffic regulations two private vehicles collided at 10.45 a.m. at the junction of Franz Schubert and Schumann Streets a woman driver was seriously injured fields of summer clouds the classical coastline of the clouds cloud contours cloud sails watermarks on the empty noon sky cloud towers of the horizon thunderclouds shadow hands the white clouds of night cloud-white cloud topography one big union man one man big union big man one union big one man union crane top blue forest noon heat of June peat smell 30 degrees in the shade tar spots in the noon sunshine

the pattern of cock-crows in the black valley the distribution of cock-crows in the black valley crossing and variation of cock-crows in the black valley squares of mail delivery vans painted yellow two tram drivers in conversation orange cleaning trucks of the Stuttgart Tramlines Co. rubble overgrown with creepers in the midst of it squadrons of swans the drifting of summer clouds useless conversations capsules rattling one against the other freely moving wind the whip of the freely moving stroke the paper pressed against the fence symbols of the world of the dead summer rhythms the sudden thunderstorms the lamp patterns of nights June clouds at that time June clouds now singing in the June night by now the situation has reached the point again where blue forest noon heat of June peat smell 30 degrees in the shade tar spots in the noon sunshine owing to non-observance of the traffic regulations two private vehicles collided at 10.45 a.m. at the junction of Franz Schubert and Schumann Streets a woman driver was seriously injured vertically fleeing shadow on a white wall to be here means only that one can remember that one can remember it means to be here crane top to be here means only that one can remember that one can remember it means to be here evening sky above the hillside woods the spherical trees of Karl Walser the conical trees of Kate Greenaway flat polished high scribbled horizon horizontal on the horizon of on the horizon of making Zschocke democraticus the

spherical trees of Karl Walser the conical trees of Kate Greenaway fields of summer clouds the classical coastline of the clouds cloud contours cloud sails watermarks on the empty noon sky cloud towers of the horizon thunderclouds shadow hands the white clouds of night cloud-white cloud topography reminds him of something that reminds him of something reminds him of something that reminds him of a girl smells rising up relapse into risen smells a room at Uhlenhorst reddish-blue tints of wet posters orange cleaning trucks of the Stuttgart Tramlines Co. rising smells relapse into risen smells a room at Uhlenhorst the pattern of cock-crows in the black valley the distribution of cock-crows in the black valley crossing and variation of cock-

crows in the black valley movements across the whole sky vertically fleeing shadow on a white wall standing to have fallen think standing to have fallen noon heat in June peat smell 30 degrees in the shade tar spots in the noon sunshine the transition consists in that one could demonstrate the wastefulness and so to speak the folly of the capitalist world by the methods of eccentric art in its sceptical relationship to general convention satisfaction of the wind on C roads [country lanes] satisfaction of memory on C roads [country lanes] one big union man one man big union big man one union big one man union squares of mail delivery vans painted yellow two tram drivers in conversation the transition consists in that one could demonstrate the wastefulness and so to speak the folly of the capitalist world by the methods of eccentric art in its sceptical relationship to general convention flat polished high scribbled horizon horizontal on the horizon of on the horizon of making

GERMANY 1944

are you attached to life they sacrifice it with fervour for higher things no one forced them to do it but their heart's beat their soul's command are you attached to life they sacrifice it with fervour for higher things no one forced them to do it but their heart's beat their soul's command the long duration of the war has led to a general slackening of rigorous views on the perniciousness of supplementary benefits for compatriots blood now circulate rejuvenated by ever more blooming bodies sweet is the body's music words are a mosaic which means that cracks run between them these logically considered are gaps one must reject and eject these vilest creatures who have ever worn the military uniform of history this rabble that has managed to save itself

from the former era I was standing now at the window now on the meadow so as to impress upon myself now this now that impression like someone who is occupied with a long sequence of camera shots perhaps much later when all these terrible things are past someone will understand the torture and the scream the front in these weeks calls only for reinforcement and weapons and the people desire to bring the very last to the front to avert the threat from our frontiers one most remarkable thing is the great growth of interest in all sorts of prophecies about the further progress of the war clairvoyants astrologers gypsies as well as cabbalistic number and letter symbolism have lately become especially widespread again blood now circulate rejuvenated by ever more blooming bodies sweet is the body's music sexual intercourse with members of alien races in the élite corps is a common occurrence one reason for it being that the reinforcement units and similar bodies employ much auxiliary personnel of alien races and more than once this had led to the institution of something almost the concubine to which must be added that the problem is also seen as connected with the problem of paragraph 175 she heard the sweat of the dying splash the long duration of the war has led to a general slackening of rigorous views on the perniciousness of supplementary benefits for compatriots for it is always moving to find this trustfulness in plain uncomplicated persons and we have to keep this weapon polished as no other weapon we cannot attain this end by quiet with excuses and reassurances when they ask us with excuses throwing sand in people's eyes as long as possible by keeping them we ourselves do not believe we plant corn and lilies in the ashes and ivy in the shadow of our swords we gather March clouds over ancient fallow ground as I write all this down I am so overwhelmed once more by the monstrosity of these things that I feel I must awaken from a bad dream the question was put to us how it is with women and children I have resolved to find a very clear solution in this matter also for I did not consider myself justified in exterminating the men read killing or having killed and leaving their avengers in the shape of child-

ren to grow up for our sons and grandsons the hard decision had to be taken to obliterate this people from the face of the earth and I stood now at the window now in the meadow to impress upon myself now this now that impression like someone who is occupied with a long sequence of camera shots in which connection it should be pointed out to the Reich Ministry of Economics that to this day enormous quantities of rags taken from non-utilizable civilian clothes remaining from the various actions at Auschwitz and other camps have been delivered and continue to be delivered we must not give these people the slightest intimation and that cannot otherwise be avoided in this pigsty of a place she heard the sweat of the dying splash the popula-

tion wavers between the oppressive fear that worse is still to come and the quiet hope that all will suddenly change in our favour must reject and eject these vilest creatures who have ever worn the military uniform of history this rabble that has managed to save itself from the former era one most remarkable thing is the great growth of interest in all sorts of prophecies about the further progress of the war clairvoyants astrologers gypsies as well as cabbalistic number and letter symbolism have lately become especially widespread again perhaps much later when all these terrible things are past someone will understand the torture and the scream are you attached to life they sacrifice it with fervour for higher things no one forced them to do it but their heart's beat their soul's command here the nation is fighting for its life and just as the individual's life depends for its being or not being on the outcome of this war so it must be implemented with all its might for this struggle we shall fight by the Rhine if necessary that makes no difference at all we shall wage war in all circumstances up to the moment when as Frederick the Great said one of our damned opponents tires of fighting on we shall fight by the Rhine if necessary that makes no difference at all we shall wage this war in all circumstances up to the moment when as Frederick the Great said one of our damned opponents tires of fighting for if we were once to loosen these bonds then rest assured of it within one

generation and in a short time everything would sink back into its old meaninglessness perhaps much later when all these terrible things are past someone will understand the torture and the scream the commanders of units on active service will decide on tactical proposals at their own responsibility and give orders accordingly to the commando forces one should not look at these things from petty egotistical points of view but must bear in mind the totality of the German race that has its karma too blood now circulate rejuvenated by ever more blooming bodies sweet is the body's music conversations too about how long it will take the German to get this shooting booth puppet off his neck the shield lowered to the ground

the sword broken into pieces naked the long duration of the war has led to a general slackening of rigorous views on the perniciousness of supplementary benefits for compatriots twentieth of July 1944 in Normandy the enemy continued his attacks in the area east and southeast of Caen with strong anti-tank and fighter support the whole day long without achieving the desired break-through after intense battles that raged all day long in St.-Lô the ruins of the cities were given up enemy advances from the city to the south as well as powerful local attacks by the Americans to the northwest broke down with heavy losses the reprisal bombardment of London continued all night North-American bomber squadrons carried out terror raids on West South-west and South Germany especially in the residential districts of the cities Munich Koblenz Schweinfurt and Saarbrücken damage occurred the population suffered losses in that action 61 aircraft were brought down by anti-aircraft forces Charon's black boat will reach no other shore where the bright Hours no rosy garland bore she heard the sweat of the dying splash the question was put to us how it was with the women and children I have resolved to find a very clear solution in this matter also for I did not consider myself justified in exterminating the men read killing or having killed and leaving their avengers in the shape of children to grow up for our sons and grandsons the hard decision had to be taken to obliterate this people from the face of the

earth to insure in the first instance within the German people's community that every good potentiality in every compatriot will develop unhindered and every achievement receive its full reward for ultimately only in this way can bolshevism and communism be overcome and that preserved on which the West depends namely the individual as a personality and if these bonds were once to loosen then rest assured of it within one generation and in a short time everything would sink back into its old meaninglessness some people offer up prayer few provisions very few lodging it is good for me to be in the city that is suffering the most air attacks twice last night I couldn't sleep anyway but lay awake thinking as often now how all these things came about

hope to describe it one day one should not look at these things from a petty egotistical point of view but must bear in mind the totality of the German race that has its karma too the uranium atom which the scientists succeeded in splitting permits us to envisage the possibility of releasing so many energies by the continuous impact of neutrons on uranium atoms that the planets could be involved in catastrophes we plant corn and lilies in the ashes and ivy in the shadow of our swords we gather March clouds over ancient fallow ground some people offer up prayer few provisions and very few lodging it is good for me to be in the city that is suffering the most air attacks twice last night I couldn't sleep anyway but lay awake thinking as often now how all these things came about hope to describe it one day the question was put to us how it was with the women and children I have resolved to find a very clear solution in this matter also for I did not consider myself justified in exterminating the men read killing or having killed and leaving their avengers in the shape of children to grow up for our sons and grandsons the hard decision had to be taken to obliterate this people from the face of this earth she heard the sweat of the dying splash the uranium atom which the scientists succeeded in splitting permits us to envisage the possibility of releasing so many energies by the continuous impact of neutrons on uranium atoms that the planets could be involved in catastrophes the question was

put to us how it was with the women and children I have resolved to find a very clear solution in this matter also for I did not consider myself justified in exterminating the men read killing or having killed and leaving their avengers in the shape of children to grow up for our sons and grandsons the hard decision had to be taken to obliterate this people from the face of the earth she heard the sweat of the dying splash she heard the sweat of the dying splash

FROM *OCCASIONAL POEMS AND BLURBS*

OCCASIONAL POEM NO. 6
AN ANTIGONE FOR HAP GRIESHABER 15/2/1969

Creon
Creon
cryin'?
cryin'? Creon cryin'?

april is the cruellest month
april is too late
mixing memory and desire
who where? is

not the growing green of his aging
snow walls with black spots
sad in hotel rooms in winter
clouds how we're accustomed to clouds

what's wrong with Creon then?
april cryin' cryin'
above how we're accustomed to clouds
a heap of broken images

but dada has never died
dada defines us
Antigone is dada
cying out against against out-crying

FROM *THE SPLITTING OF THE CABBAGE*

MAX IMMEDIATELY BEFORE FALLING ASLEEP
PROGRESSION IN 0+21 BEATS

0
Max 3
> immediately before falling asleep he still considers at what moment immediately before falling asleep he will cease to consider whether immediately before falling asleep he will consider at what moment immediately before falling asleep he will cease to consider

Narrator
> at last Mr. Gillyflore too lay down to sleep in his head there was an uproar a banging a ringing his senses began to grow dull he made one more effort to think of something interesting to make some important decision in a very ticklish business to arrive at some sort of judgement but couldn't any more sleep enfolded his head and so he fell fast asleep as people do who are not used to drinking but in friendly company have been persuaded to empty a glass or two

1
Max 2
> hardly has he closed the door when she hurls herself upon him hardly has she closed the door when he hurls himself upon her hardly have I closed the door when they hurl themselves upon me hardly have we closed the door when we hurl ourselves upon one another

Commentator A
> I wish to make the acquaintance of an educated kindly honest affectionate person

Commentator B
> Paris discovers industrial reforms

2
Max 3
> when suddenly there will be nothing left and all that is left has been used up and all that has been accumulated has to be discounted and nothing remains to be done indeed doing itself ceases as that which was left

Max 2
> to keep a tight grip on one buttock

Commentator A
> for now or later wanted an efficient experienced head secretary

Commentator B
> bread for the world

Interjector
> Max pushes his hat back from his forehead and says it's all hogwash

Narrator
> often something compels me to do something I think unreasonable I am inclined to spend a long time thinking about humiliating experiences and often I have to go and look to see whether the door is locked or the light has been switched off I often have to count up in my head things I have seen often ask myself whether I did the right thing I often have bad words in my head and can't get rid of them

3
Max 1
> to that extent the whole of me perceived confronts my simple self-awareness and since the former is thus the thing distinguished it is distinguished in my pure conception in time and into the content or into the thing-in-itself but as its subject substance has the primal inner necessity by which in itself to present itself as that which intrinsically I am

Max 2
> to keep a tight grip on one buttock

4
Max 3
> it gave me a great deal of pleasure but when the pleasure that gave so much pleasure stops it doesn't give so much pleasure and everything that still gives pleasure now is thinking that perhaps one day it will give pleasure again still

Commentator A
> wanted foreign correspondent sport-loving pretty girl charming lady tutor requires sales consultant

Commentator B
> nitrogen gasps for air

Interjector
> Max sits down at the round table

Narrator
> I have the impression that my thoughts are quite normal but sometimes I have strange thoughts that I can't get rid of I am prey to the strangest thoughts and fancies I am afraid to be alone because I am always prey to the strangest thoughts and fancies

5
Max 1
> as I look the negative in the eye linger upon it this lingering is the magic force that transmutes it into being it is the subject which in that it gives existence to the determinedness in its element is the true substance which does not have its mediation outside me but is that mediation itself

Max 2
> I squeeze my face into the flesh of her thighs

Interjector
> Max sits down at the round table

Narrator
> fear is not the curtain that divided us from action but it constitutes a part of the action itself and when we speak of forsakenness we only mean to say that God does not exist and one must draw the ultimate conclusions from that fact

6
Max 2
> he grasps her two buttocks with one hand her behind quivers

Commentator A
> wanted managing secretary

Commentator B
> the weather at the weekend the weather on Thursday

Interjector
> Max puts his glass on the table and says I must say

Narrator
> often I feel afraid other people might think I am unintelligent or uneducated often I suddenly feel afraid there's something wrong with my stuff often I feel afraid of behaving in a ridiculous way

7
Max 2
> I feel it growing stiff and I feel myself growing stiff

Narrator
> I'm afraid of snakes I'm afraid of water I feel afraid in the dark I feel afraid in crowded places I'm afraid of spiders I feel afraid when I suddenly find myself in a confined closed space

8
Max 2
> he look at the fleshy lips between the dense curly hair my diaphragm quivers

Commentator A
> very good-looking lady the dream woman requires lady buyer sport-loving plump

Commentator B
> the revision of the laws governing sexual conduct is turning into a test case

Interjector
> to come from Wuppertal and return there via Rio that takes some imagining says Max

9
Max 1
> so it is this general need of human beings to seek in their minds in that it is a manner of bringing home to a human being what he or she is

Max 2
> she thrusts her hand under her right leg for his testicles

Commentator A
> wanted a visitor of lady doctors

Interjector
> there you are says Max

Narrator
> Janet Taylor put together a graded questionnaire based on the items of the Minnesota Multiphasic Personality Inventory these were selected with the approval of five experimental psychologists as being connected with manifest fear

10
Max 3
> I have mucked around a good deal with a good deal of pleasure with a good many things and yet discovered a good many things that give a good deal of trouble and which necessarily contains a good deal of the things which I have been concerned with for quite a while

Max 2
> she has an extraordinarily smooth arse

Commentator A
> wanted lady supervisor of a home

Commentator B
> rounded-off chemical corporations

Narrator
> if one studies the fear that expresses itself in the form of specific neurotic symptoms one seems to obtain a general factor of fear in every specific case that is in the case of phobic fear fear of separation fear of castration that is in case of social fear social shyness fear of exposing oneself and fear of revealing one's inferiority

11
Max 3
> whether I thought anything of it and when I thought anything of it or whether what I thought of it is the same as what I should have thought of it if I had thought nothing of it

Max 2
> I squeeze my face into the flesh of her thighs

Narrator
> almost I am not sad I am sad am sad all the time can't do anything about it am so sad that it hurts am so sad that I can't bear it any more

12
Interjector
> of my Max my Max my Max your legs are like wax like wax like wax

Narrator
> only at times I worry about my health I am always worried by sickness and pain my physical condition worries me so much that it's hard for me to think of anything else my physical condition takes up all my time and energy

13
Max 2
> she unbuttons my trousers and takes hold of my penis and moves her hand up and down fast

Interjector
> and what will people say when I'm in Rio hallo Max people will say

Narrator
> fear can arise spontaneously or provoked by certain circumstances and although phobic fear must be regarded as provoked fear induced by an object or by a situation it remains pathological because of its irrational nature

14
Max 3
> now as far as play is concerned it concerns playing and as far as playing is concerned it concerns the player and now as far as the player is concerned that concerns the question what game the player is playing what game is that player playing

Max 2
> to lick the seam of the scrotum

Commentator A
> wanted au-pair girl

Commentator B
> three nuns drowned

Interjector
> Max pushes the ashtray away and calls out hallo

15
Max 2
> I take off her slip and push up her suspender belt and hurl myself open-mouthed on to

Commentator A
> wanted emancipated lady with initiative

Commentator B
> locked-in ladies in Panama protest

Narrator
> in any event fear is not only a matter of feeling a person feels something and is not afraid in some separate compartment of his make-up but fear possesses him completely he is fear

16/17
Max 1
> this consciousness then has not experienced fear about this or that at this or that moment but about its entire existence for it has felt the fear of death of the absolute Lord it has been dissolved in it inwardly has trembled thoroughly within itself and all that was firm in it was shaken

Max 2
> hardly has he closed the door when she hurls herself upon him he thrusts his middle finger into her arsehole hardly has she closed the door when he hurls himself upon her hardly have they closed the door when we hurl ourselves upon each other he rubs her clitoris between thumb and middle finger

Interjector
> Max rocks his white arse bang bang

Narrator
> commonly floating fear is distinguished from fixed fear and our concern here is with that floating fear which has no other object any more than death

18
Commentator A
> wanted intelligent emancipated cheerful personality

Commentator B
> decision on merger due soon

Narrator
> always a particular thought pursues me and I can't get rid of it always the same thought pursues me the same thought pursues me so relentlessly that I can't focus my mind on anything else

19/20
Max 2
> hardly has he closed the door when she hurls herself upon him pulls off her skirt pants suspender belt with one jerk as she bends over his hand slips between her buttocks she is completely moist hardly have we closed the door when I hurl myself upon her I pull off her skirt pants suspender belt with one jerk my hand slips

    between her thighs she is completely moist
Interjector
    Max rocks his white arse bang bang

21
Max 1
    as subject I am the pure simple negativity and for that very reason the splitting of what was simple or the opposing duplication which in turn is the negation of this indifferent diversity
Max 2
    I grasp her two buttocks with one hand her behind quivers
Commentator A
    wanted lady supervisor for a home
Commentator B
    foxes are not suffering distress
Interjector
    hallo Max where are the others
Max 3
    immediately before falling asleep Max hears distant piano music the excessively loud ticking of an alarm clock distant chimes of a church clock distant singing in the night close footfalls in the street distant aircraft noise excessively loud buzzing of a fly the sound of his own heartbeat the sound of his own breathing nearby the barking of a dog nearby the noise of a passing car excessively loud the sound of rain on leaves nearby the sound of a blind coming down loud the sound of rain on leaves distantly the noise of a passing car distant barking of dogs excessively loud the sound of his own breathing excessively loud the sound of his own heartbeat nearby buzzing of flies distant aircraft noise nearby footfalls in the street distant singing in the night and scraps of music distant chiming of church clocks nearby the ticking of an alarm clock nearby the chiming of church clocks distant singing in the night footfalls in the street aircraft noise fly noise rain on leaves his own heartbeat his own breathing the sudden passing of a car etc.